MORAL VALUE
AND
HUMAN DIVERSITY

MORAL VALUE
AND
HUMAN DIVERSITY

Robert Audi

OXFORD
UNIVERSITY PRESS

2007

OXFORD
UNIVERSITY PRESS

Oxford University Press, Inc., publishes works that further
Oxford University's objective of excellence
in research, scholarship, and education.

Oxford   New York
Auckland   Cape Town   Dar es Salaam   Hong Kong   Karachi
Kuala Lumpur   Madrid   Melbourne   Mexico City   Nairobi
New Delhi   Shanghai   Taipei   Toronto

With offices in
Argentina   Austria   Brazil   Chile   Czech Republic   France   Greece
Guatemala   Hungary   Italy   Japan   Poland   Portugal   Singapore
South Korea   Switzerland   Thailand   Turkey   Ukraine   Vietnam

Copyright © 2007 by Oxford University Press, Inc.

Published by Oxford University Press, Inc.
198 Madison Avenue, New York, New York 10016

www.oup.com

Oxford is a registered trademark of Oxford University Press

Library of Congress Cataloging-in-Publication Data

Audi, Robert, 1941–
Moral value and human diversity / Robert Audi.
p. cm.
Includes bibliographical references and index.
ISBN 978-0-19-531294-2
1. Ethical relativism.   2. Culture—Moral and ethical aspects.   3. Multiculturalism—
Moral and ethical aspects.   4. Ethics.   5. Values.   I. Title.
BJ37.A93 2007
170—dc22   2006050325

3 5 7 9 8 6 4 2

Printed in the United States of America
on acid-free paper

To my brother and sister

PREFACE

The present age is marked by an ominous tension. Human diversity has never been so prominent, and the need for co-operation among utterly different people has never been so urgent. Differences in culture, education, ethnicity, religion, and lifestyles easily divide people. Can ethics provide standards of conduct that give everyone a sense of inherent worth and make it possible to resolve conflicts peacefully? This is a hope of most major writers in ethics. But they, too, differ among themselves, and their disagreements have, in many people, reduced confidence that ethics can provide standards we can all use in guiding our lives and our relations with others.

This book describes the most influential kinds of ethical views and, without neglecting their differences, draws on what they have in common to formulate moral standards that can help with some of the major challenges now facing us—individually and as societies. I divide these views into four categories. One category is the kind of virtue ethics found in Aristotle. The other three categories comprise three kinds of rule-based ethics: the moral theory of Immanuel Kant, the utilitarianism represented by John Stuart Mill, and the common-sense ethics that is associated with the intuitionism of W. D. Ross, though its origins go back at least to Aquinas.

The major proponents of these ethical views (all of which may have been also articulated in some version outside the philosophy of the Western Hemisphere) did not put them forward with the acute consciousness of human differences that is needed in the contemporary world. I will present the views with this in mind. Doing this requires considering "relativism," a term used in ways that easily confuse. One way I clarify ethical relativism is by indicating some of the ways in which, despite appearances, ethics is like science. In this light I will show that major ethical views are universally applicable but also have a kind of relativity to circumstance that provides a degree of flexibility they have commonly been thought to lack.

Ethics has always been taken to concern both the good and the bad (the realm of value) and the right and the wrong (the realm of obligation). A well-developed ethical view should indicate how these two realms are related. This is largely a matter of how what we ought to do is connected with how we can live a good life. That question, in turn, is central for the theory of value. Most of what we do presupposes judgments of one or another kind of value. What kinds of judgments are these? And what sorts of things really have value? I am especially interested in what has value in a sense important for diverse people regardless of their particular culture or outlook.

The first part of the book takes up virtue ethics, Kantian ethics, utilitarianism, and common-sense intuitionism and formulates a broad ethical position that draws on all of these four kinds of view. It also proposes a conception of value that is readily integrated with that broad position. The second part of the book indicates how the ethical views introduced in part I might structure the kinds of lives people might lead regardless of major differences between them. This takes the reader beyond general and theoretical ethics into practical ethics. The final chapter goes a good distance into political philosophy and addresses some problems of applied

ethics. It considers a number of ethical challenges we face
today.

All of the ethical views examined in part I can be applied
to these contemporary challenges, but I naturally give promi-
nence to the bearing of my own position in dealing with
them. In a short book, however, it is enough to provide the
basis for dealing with these and related challenges. Solving
the problems is more than any single book can do.

In writing a short, non-technical book I have had to omit
much that I would have liked to include, especially elaboration
of the ethical views presented, discussion of relevant literature,
analysis of argument and counterargument, and citations of
data concerning the ethical challenges detailed in part II.
Some of the gaps are filled in works referred to in the notes.
But my hope is that the book says enough to make compre-
hension easy for those coming to ethics and political philosophy with little or no background in them, and that it is written
with sufficient comprehensiveness and care to make it valuable for those with long experience in these fields.

I have also designed the book so that those interested
mainly in general ethics can concentrate on part I, which is
self-contained. Part II, if not entirely self-contained, can be
read without study of part I and can certainly be taught separately by instructors familiar with the main ethical positions
presented in part I and preferring to emphasize the questions
of social and political philosophy prominent in part II. General readers and students in introductory college courses can
understand the book throughout; and instructors in those
courses can extend the discussions, in relation to their own
ethical views, in ways that should be fruitful for both their
teaching and their own work.

ACKNOWLEDGMENTS

This book grew out of the A. C. Reid Lectures delivered at Wake Forest University in the spring of 2001. The first chapter, however, had already been drafted for an earlier lecture at Colgate University. A later version of all of the chapters was presented at Santa Clara University, where both the Markkula Center for Applied Ethics and the Department of Philosophy hosted a series of seminars in which the chapters were discussed in detail with great benefit to my thinking on many of the topics. Discussions on those occasions and on other occasions when I presented some of the ideas were of great value to me in thinking about the main questions. I cannot even begin to name all of the friends, students, fellow philosophers, and critical audiences whose responses to one or another idea in the book has helped me, but some colleagues provided immensely valuable comments on earlier drafts. For comments and helpful discussion I particularly want to thank Karl Ameriks, Jerome Balmuth, Roger Crisp, David De-Cosse, Georges Enderle, James Felt, S.J., Bernard Gert, Kent Greenawalt, Kirk Hanson, Brad Hooker, Jonathan Jacobs, Lynn Joy, Philip Kain, Stephen Kalish, Ralph Kennedy, Janet Kourany, Christopher Kulp, Scott LaBarge, Win-chiat Lee, David McCabe, Michael Meyer, Paolo Monti, Patrick E. Murphy, Lawrence Nelson, Michael Perry, William Prior, Elizabeth Radcliffe, Walter Sinnott-Armstrong, David Solomon,

James Sterba, Lee Tavis, Ann Tenbrunsel, Mark Timmons, Peter van Inwagen, David Weinstein, Oliver Williams, C.S.C., Nicholas Wolterstorff, Patrick Yarnell, and, especially, Christian Miller and Peter Wicks, who both made extensive comments and suggestions on an earlier draft. I am also grateful to Peter Ohlin and others at Oxford University Press—especially Linda Donnelly and Lara Zoble—for advice and help in the process of design and production and to Norma McLemore for copyediting.

CONTENTS

PART I   MAJOR ETHICAL VIEWS AND
          THE DIMENSIONS OF VALUE

1 Ethical Theory and the Moral Fragmentation
  of Modern Life   3

   1 Some Major Types of Ethical View   5
   2 Toward Ethical Integration   16
   3 Ethics and Science: Beyond the Stereotypes   21
   4 Relativism and Objectivity   24
   5 Ten Challenges for Contemporary Ethics   28

2 The Experience of Value: What Do We Value,
  and Why Should We Care?   35

   1 Value Versus Valuation   36
   2 The Good and the True   38
   3 The Primacy of Experience   39
   4 The Multiple Dimensions of Value   41
   5 Moral Value   47
   6 The Organic Character of Value   49
   7 Fact and Value   52

PART II   HUMAN DIVERSITY AND THE ETHICAL
          CHALLENGES OF CONTEMPORARY LIFE

3 Moral Pluralism and Cultural Relativity   59

   1 The Diversity of Value   59
   2 Human Sociality   62
   3 The Plurality of Integrated Lives   65
   4 The Challenge of Cultural Differences and
     Clashing World Views   78

4 Human Diversity and Democratic Institutions   83
    1 The Nature of Institutions   84
    2 Institutional Ethics in Pluralistic Democracies   87
    3 Institutional Citizenship and Political Responsibility 88
    4 News Media   89
    5 A Framework for Approaching Moral Problems
       in Free Democracies   91

Conclusion   119

Notes   123

Index   141

PART I

MAJOR ETHICAL VIEWS AND
THE DIMENSIONS OF VALUE

1

ETHICAL THEORY AND THE MORAL FRAGMENTATION OF MODERN LIFE

We live in a world of pervasive threats to peace, violence in homes and schools, global warming and environmental plunder, fraud and incompetence, fast-growing population in some poor countries and starvation in others, and rapid obsolescence in what we build. In many tasks, even people themselves have become obsolete. The advanced technology by which we aim to make life better has eliminated jobs that many once counted on and has contributed to a steep rise in the cost of health care. It has rendered almost all of us subject to replacement by machines in part of what we do. Technological efforts to improve our world have made life more difficult for many of us and more dangerous for all of us.

The contemporary world poses at least two major challenges to ethics. One of them is practical: to provide principles and ideals to guide us in dealing with the problems just described. We need sound standards for personal, institutional, and international conduct. The other challenge to ethics is theoretical. It derives in part from the naturalistic worldview commonly thought to be supported by the progress of science, the view that the natural word (the universe conceived as containing no supernatural beings) is the whole of reality and that scientific method is the only reliable route to general knowledge of reality. This naturalism seems to leave no place for value: for what is intrinsically good or intrinsically bad. Science is in fact supposed to be "value free,"[1] to make no judgments of value beyond those warranted by its own internal standards of evidence used to assess claims to truth in terms of scientific acceptability.

Even for those who do not share the common commitment to the intellectual sovereignty of science as providing the only reliable routes to knowledge of human nature and our world, it is easy to be skeptical about values. Values cannot be *seen*. We can see a good painting, but its goodness is not like its colors and shapes and may evade many viewers. Similarly, we may see someone do a morally good deed, but its moral goodness is not a visible property of the bodily movements that meet the eye. Nor is value quantitatively measurable, or required for scientific descriptions and explanations.[2] How, then, can we reasonably affirm standards of the right and the good as any more than projections of our own preferences? How is it even possible to find ideals for human life that we can all respect despite our many individual and cultural differences and in the absence of a scientific case for their soundness?

In the light of these and other ethical challenges soon to be described, some sensitive observers of the contemporary world may feel alienated, disoriented, and anxious. William Butler Yeats strikingly foreshadowed these attitudes in "The Second Coming." It begins:

> Turning and turning in the widening gyre
> The falcon cannot hear the falconer;
> Things fall apart; the centre cannot hold;
> Mere anarchy is loosed upon the world,
> The blood-dimmed tide is loosed, and everywhere
> The ceremony of innocence is drowned;
> The best lack all conviction, while the worst
> Are full of passionate intensity.[3]

My aim is to say something about the practical and theoretical problems I have sketched. I begin by outlining some of the basic resources available to us from ethics ("moral philosophy," in an older terminology).

Normative ethics—the kind I mainly want to discuss—has traditionally considered chiefly three related questions. First, *the character question*: what is a morally good person? More specifically, What character traits are moral *virtues*? Second, *the conduct question*: What ought we to *do*, especially in distributing benefits and burdens among us—say, health care and military responsibilities—and in regulating our conduct? Third, *the value question*: What things in life are *good as ends*, worth seeking for their own sake and not just as means to something else? Our view of these goods will largely determine the kind and content of the education we support. It will also influence what we *care* about.

Let's start with four kinds of normative view that derive, respectively, from stress on these three practical questions: the questions of the kind of character we should have, of what deeds we should do, and of what in human life is good.

1. Some Major Types of Ethical View

There are more kinds of ethical views than I can consider, but the four to be sketched can be extended and combined in various ways and, singly or in combination, provide a basis for understanding many other positions in ethics. They also give us a good basis for understanding the resources of ethical reflection in general, conceived as a framework for guiding the solution of myriad contemporary problems.

Virtue Ethics

Among the most acclaimed ethical views are *virtue theories*. These demand that one concentrate on being a good—a virtuous—person. Be honest, just, kind, and honorable, for instance. Plato and Aristotle developed views of this sort, and they are currently held in many forms. Aristotle described (for instance) just acts as the kind that a just person would perform; a just person is not to be defined as one who performs just acts.[4] Aristotle apparently took moral traits of character to be ethically more basic than moral acts. He said, for instance, regarding the types of acts that are right, "Actions are called just or temperate when they are the sort that a just or temperate person would do" (*Nicomachean Ethics* 1105b5ff). It is virtues, such as justice and temperance, rather than acts, that are ethically central for Aristotle: "Virtue makes us aim at the right target, and practical wisdom makes us use the right means" (1144a).

For a virtue ethics, agents and their traits, as opposed to rules of action, are morally basic. The idea is that we are to understand what it is to behave justly through studying the nature and tendencies of the just person, not the other way around. We do not, for instance, construct a notion of just deeds as those that treat people equally, and then define a just person as one who characteristically does deeds of this sort. Thus, for adults as well as for children, and in ordinary life as in the professions, role models are absolutely crucial for moral learning. The person of practical wisdom is the chief role model in ethics; such people exemplify all of the moral virtues and also tend to be good advisors in ethical decisions.

Aristotle understood the virtues in the context of his theory of the good for human beings. He says of this good, "the best good must be something complete," and he takes only happiness (*flourishing* in some translations) to meet this condition:

> Now happiness more than anything else seems complete [since "choiceworthy in its own right"] without qualification. For we always choose it because of itself, never because of something else. Honor, pleasure, understanding and every virtue we certainly choose because of themselves, since we would choose each of them even if it had no

further result, but also choose them for the sake of happiness, supposing that through them we shall be happy. (1097a–b5)

Happiness, then, stands as our final unifying end: we may seek other things for their own sake, but only when "through them" we can achieve happiness. Happiness is not, however, a passive state. It requires a life in which "actions and activities . . . that involve reason" (which is our distinctive characteristic) is central; the "human good," then, proves to be activity of the soul [roughly, mind] in accord with virtue" (1098b214–17).

If, however, we take traits as ethically more basic than acts, we face a problem: how does a virtue theory tell us what to *do*? Ethics largely concerns *conduct*. How do we figure out what counts as, for instance, being generous or honorable? Virtue ethics has resources for answering this, including the appeal to practical wisdom as applied to the context of decision. A person of practical wisdom is a paradigm of one having virtue, and in a famous passage Aristotle calls virtue "a state that decides, consisting of a mean, the mean relative to us, which is defined by reason. . . . It is a mean between two vices, one of excess and one of deficiency" (1107a1–4). Consider beneficence. If, relative to my resources, I am selfish and ignore others' needs, this is a deficiency; if I give so much at once that I am prevented from doing much more for others later, I am excessive. Good ethical decisions, on this view, may be seen in the light of such comparisons. There is, however, a contrasting approach that takes acts to be ethically more basic than virtues of character. The contrast helps to clarify both approaches.

Rule Ethics

Rule theories—probably now the dominant kind of view in ethics—generally hold that the primary task of ethics is to

provide the right rules of action, though rule theorists generally grant that the cultivation of virtue is important and must
begin early in childhood. For rule theories, only when we
know the rules that govern, say, generous and honorable conduct can we teach or cultivate the virtue of generosity and
honor.

Divine Command Ethics

There are several major kinds of rule views. Among the oldest
and most widely accepted is the divine command view. It says,
in part, that what we morally ought to do is follow the rules
laid down by God.[5] The Ten Commandments (Exodus 20:
1–17) and Jesus' love commandments (Matthew 22: 37–39)
and Sermon on the Mount (Matthew 5–7) are the most famous representations of divinely ordained moral principles.
The former set, at least, contains a sort of elementary moral
code. Its moral requirements prohibit killing, lying, stealing,
greed, and adultery.[6] The love commandments add (among
other things) the highly demanding injunction to love one's
neighbor as oneself.

More detailed codes of conduct can be derived from either set of commandments. That derivation is no routine exercise, however. Consider how difficult it can be to say when
lawyers advocating for their clients are "bearing false witness." They need not lie to present a biased picture, for instance by destroying the credibility of a truthful witness or by
magnifying the importance of true but misleading statements
by some other witness.

As important as divine command ethics is in certain major
religious traditions, it is normally tied to a particular religion in
a way that prevents its being a universal resource in the way the
other ethical positions considered in this book can be. Moreover, it is commonly connected with those other positions in
constructive ways, and many of its characteristic requirements

coincide with theirs. In part II, it will be taken into account as we consider the integration of ethical and religious perspectives, but we will concentrate on the other positions.

Kantian Ethics

A second famous rule theory is that of the great eighteenth-century philosopher Immanuel Kant. His master principle, the Categorical Imperative, says, in one formulation, that we are always to act in such a way that we can rationally will the principle we are acting on to be a universal law:

> Act as if the maxim of your action [roughly the principle underlying it] were to become through your will a universal law of nature. (422)[7]

Thus, I should not leave someone to bleed to death on the roadside if I could not rationally will the universality of the practice—say, even when *I* am the victim. We would not want to universalize, and thus live by, the callous principle: One should stop for someone bleeding to death provided it requires no self-sacrifice. Similarly, I should not make a lying promise to repay money if I could not rationally universalize the underlying principle (say, When I can get money only by making a lying promise to repay it, I will do this). One way to see why the imperative apparently disallows this principle is to note that I count on sincere promises from others and cannot rationally endorse the universality of a deceitful practice that would victimize me.

Kant also gave a less abstract formulation of the Categorical Imperative:

> Act in such a way that you always treat humanity, whether in your own person or in the person of any other, never simply as a means, but always at the same time as an end. (429)

The requirement is that we always treat persons not merely as means, but also as ends in themselves. In part, the imperative seems to say: Never *use* people, as in manipulatively lying to them; instead, respect them. Treating people as ends clearly requires caring about their good. They matter as persons, and one must to some extent act *for their sake* whether or not one benefits from it.[8]

This formulation applies to oneself as well as others; it requires a kind of respect for persons, and this includes self-respect. If we take Kant's two formulations together (and he considered them equivalent), then apparently we must not only treat persons as ends but—as the rational universalizability of our principles would suggest—*equally* so. Everyone matters and matters equally.

Utilitarianism

A third kind of rule theory is suggested by the question: what *good* are rules unless they contribute to our well-being—unless (above all) following them enhances human happiness and reduces human suffering? This kind of concern leads to *utilitarianism*, the position of Jeremy Bentham and John Stuart Mill. For Mill (the greatest English nineteenth-century philosopher), the master principle is roughly this: Choose that act from among your options which is best from the twin points of view of increasing human happiness and reducing human suffering. In Mill's words:

> The creed which accepts as the foundation of morals "utility" . . . holds that actions are right in proportion as they tend to promote happiness, wrong as they tend to produce the reverse of happiness. By happiness is intended pleasure, and the absence of pain.[9]

If one act produces more happiness than another, it is preferable, other things equal. If the first also produces suffering, other things are not equal. We have to weigh good consequences of our projected acts against any bad ones and subtract the negative value from the positive. Ideally, our actions would be doubly good, producing pleasure *and* reducing suffering.

The ethical aim for action is to find options second to none in total value understood in terms of happiness.[10] For instance, lying causes suffering, at least in the long run; truthfulness contributes, over time, to our well-being—roughly, how well off we are from the point of view of happiness as the positive element and suffering as the negative one. Mill argued similarly in support of other morally required conduct, such as fairness in dealing with others and non-interference with other people's conduct.

Utilitarianism is commonly formulated as the position that for an act to be morally right is for it to produce "the greatest good for the greatest number."[11] This misrepresents the view. Utilitarians are concerned above all to maximize the good. Some ways to produce good for all concerned, say by providing education for all children, are no doubt quantitatively better than others because of how many people they help; but the idea that doing (or producing) good for more people rather than fewer is not a *basic* concern of utilitarianism and is not appropriate to defining the position. For instance, if providing public libraries only in highly educated communities would produce more good (say, in stimulating innovations and productivity) than providing them equally to a whole population (where this entails their being of lower quality), the former, narrower distribution would be preferred.[12]

Common-Sense Intuitionism

Suppose one agrees with virtue theorists that there are as many different dimensions of morality as there are moral virtues, and with rule theorists in holding that morality

demands that we have and act on *principles*. This may lead
to the kind of common-sense ethical theory set out by the
twentieth-century English moral philosopher W. D. Ross. His
approach—a kind of multiple-rule view—is to categorize our
basic duties (moral obligations). He did this by considering
the kinds of grounds on which moral obligations rest; for instance, making a promise to help you weed your garden is a
ground of an obligation to do it; injuring someone in rush-
ing to a class is a ground of an obligation to make reparations; and seeing someone bleeding by the wayside, as the
Good Samaritan did (Luke 10:30–35), is a ground of an obligation to help, even if not necessarily a predominating
ground. For Ross,

> That an act *qua* [as] fulfilling a promise, or *qua* effecting
> a just distribution of good, or *qua* returning services
> rendered, or *qua* promoting the good of others, or *qua* pro-
> moting the virtue of the agent is *prima facie* right, is self-
> evident . . . in the sense that when we have reached suffi-
> cient mental maturity and have given sufficient attention
> to the proposition it is evident without any need of proof,
> or of evidence beyond itself. . . . In our confidence that
> these propositions are true there is involved the same con-
> fidence in our reason that is involved in our confidence in
> mathematics.[13]

This passage affirms moral principles expressing prima facie
obligations. For Ross the basic prima facie obligations include (as suggested here) obligations to (1) keep promises,
(2) act justly, (3) express gratitude for services rendered, and
(4) do good deeds toward others. Ross also stressed (in the
same chapter) the obligations to (5) avoid injuring others, (6)
make reparations for wrongdoing, (7) avoid lying, and (more
positively) (8) improve oneself. He considered it intuitively
clear and indeed self-evident that we have these eight obligations: you can see this by simply engaging in sufficiently clear

and deep reflection—a kind of intuitive thinking—on the moral concepts in question. Hence the name 'intuitionism' for the position that morality is to be conceived in terms of the principles expressing these commonly recognized obligations.[14]

Ross knew that prima facie obligations can conflict. Recall the Good Samaritan. He went to great lengths to help a wounded stranger. Suppose he had promised to help his daughter harvest her olives and was unable to do this given the delay caused by ministering to the stranger. Ross thought that where two or more duties (his term for obligations) conflict, we often need practical wisdom (wisdom in human affairs) to determine which duty is *final*, that is, which duty is, all things considered, the one we ought to fulfill, as opposed to our "prima facie duty," our duty relative to the moral grounds in the situation. Here the opposing moral grounds are a wounded stranger's need for one's help and a promise to one's daughter. Our final obligation is what we ought to do "in the end," and it will be the same as our prima facie obligation *if* no other such obligation of equal weight conflicts with that. If I promise to write you and have no conflicting duty, writing you is what I ought to do.

There is an Aristotelian element in Ross's common-sense ethics. Practical wisdom is what Aristotle took to be essential in determining what kinds of acts express virtue; and Ross thought, as Aristotle may have, that sometimes it is intuitive, or even obvious, which of two conflicting obligations takes precedence. Saving an injured person may be quite obviously a stronger obligation than keeping a promise to help harvest olives. By contrast, the choice of one good candidate over another good one to fill an important position may rarely be obviously right. Here morality counsels humility—and the constant retrospective self-scrutiny that helps us both to rectify past mistakes and to avoid future errors.

Some Ethical Contrasts: The Right,
the Virtuous, and the Good

To see some respects in which these basic kinds of ethical views differ, consider a case in which your grandfather (who has out-lived your parents) puts you in charge of directing his medical treatment if he becomes incompetent. You have promised to let him die with dignity if he is suffering, unable to communicate, and clearly terminally ill. His lung disease prevents normal breathing, and putting him on a respirator is suggested. He suffers when conscious, cannot communicate or even understand what is said to him, and is being fed through tubes. Many facts that such a case presents cannot be filled in here, but even at this point we can see some differences between the approaches. Take common-sense intuitionism first, since it views our promissory obligations as a morally basic kind. Unless we find some conflicting obligation of equal weight, we must do as we promised and decline to allow a respirator. Imagine, however, that other grandchildren have asked to come to him one last time and need a day to make the trip. Here one might have an obligation of beneficence—to do something good for them—that would favor a respirator if he would otherwise die too quickly. Suppose one could confine its use for this short-term purpose. Allowing its use might then be consistent with the original promise.

A virtue ethics could lead one to a similar decision. The virtue of fidelity is the one most relevant here. Fidelity to one's word is central, but the virtue is broader and encompasses loyalty to others. There is a virtue of beneficence as well, and this would incline one much as the Rossian obligation of beneficence would. One's central focus, however, would be on what kind of person to be in the situation; this conception is to lead one to the right deed. The procedure is not to consider types of action and bring rules to bear on them. It is crucial to see that as different as these approaches are, they may, like different ways of building a bridge, take one to the same destination.

The Kantian and utilitarian accounts both differ strikingly from the positions of intuitionism and virtue ethics. The former two are each what might be called *master principle theories* of right action, whereas the latter are highly *pluralistic*.[15] For the virtue approach, there is a plurality of virtues central for ethical thinking; for intuitionism, there is a plurality of rules. This is not to imply that the decision you should make must differ depending on which of the master principle views is your guide. Indeed, the Categorical Imperative is commonly taken to *imply* a subsidiary moral principle expressing a strong obligation to keep promises, as well as a principle of beneficence calling for doing good deeds. This makes it like intuitionism in a certain kind of application, and indeed utilitarians may also formulate principles far more specific than the master principle quoted from Mill and (they may argue) derivable from it. But a Kantian would likely arrive at a decision differently than would someone guided by one of the other views. We should try to think of a principle for the case that could be used by *anyone* in the same situation, for instance the principle that when a promised release from suffering and indignity can be carried out with just a slight delay by accommodating relatives with a deep and loving concern to be present, the delay is warranted. We might also ask whether the grandfather is being treated as an end and not merely a means. If we were sure he would not have agreed to a delay in such a case, we would likely not think we are treating him as an end (roughly, as mattering for his own sake); but apart from such an unlikely factor, we could reasonably think he might have wanted to have his other grandchildren present. We can then see the delay in letting him die as treating him as an end.

On the kind of utilitarian view sketched, our focus must be on the good to be done by making one decision rather than another. We might now focus on how much suffering the grandfather will endure in the extra day on the respirator and might compare that with the suffering of the grandchildren if they cannot get to him before he dies. We might also think about the effects of the example we set if we delay (or if we do not); being seen as breaking a promise can have very bad consequences. Even the pressure for hospital space and the costs of the extra medical care will be relevant for a utilitarian.

None of these things need be *irrelevant* on the other views; but for utilitarianism, facts are relevant on the basis of their bearing on the consequences of our options for the happiness of all affected, not of their bearing on whether we are keeping a promise, being virtuous, or following a rule that is universalizable in the way Kant intended. This difference in approach is enormous, though one may often reach the same moral destination on any of the approaches. On the utilitarian view, we may properly be influenced by the monetary costs much more than on the other views; we may be thinking of how much good could be done with the savings. For intuitionism, by contrast, the obligation of beneficence—which is the overarching obligation for utilitarianism—is only one important moral consideration here; the promise also has moral weight, and even an obligation of gratitude toward the grandfather may add to the grounds for adhering to the original promise.

2. Toward Ethical Integration

Two or more of these views can be fruitfully combined; for instance, you might hold that we are to maximize happiness, as Mill requires, but only *within* the limits of never treating people merely as means, as Kant demands. On this combined view, you cannot sacrifice an innocent person to harvest organs that will save six others, even if the total resulting happiness would be greater (in which case a purely utilitarian approach would call for the sacrifice).

Many who reflect on ethics find something of value in virtue ethics, in Kantianism, and in utilitarianism. Might a single wide principle capture much of their content? An approach I find promising is to combine elements in these three historically most influential theories in ethics: the virtue theory, the Kantian view, and utilitarianism. There are apparently at least three conceptually independent factors that a good ethical theory should take into account: happiness, which we may think of as welfare conceived in terms of pleasure, pain, and suffering; justice, conceived largely as requiring equal treatment of persons; and freedom. These are all reflected on the Rossian list of basic obligations, but for simplicity I leave out the others, which may in any case be justifiably affirmed on the basis of these.[16]

On this approach—call it *pluralist universalism*—our broadest moral principle would require optimizing happiness so far as possible without producing injustice or curtailing freedom (including one's own); and this principle is to be *internalized*—roughly, automatically presupposed and normally also strongly motivating—in a way that yields moral virtue. Each value becomes, then, a guiding standard, and mature moral agents will develop a sense of how to act (or at least how to reach a decision to act) when the values pull in different directions.[17]

No specific, single standard, however, can be our sole moral guide. This is especially so in the case of principles that appeal to different and potentially conflicting elements. How should we balance these? A priority rule for achieving a balance among the three values is this. Considerations of justice and freedom take priority (at least normally) over considerations of happiness; justice and freedom (presumably) do not conflict because justice requires the highest level of freedom possible within the limits of peaceful coexistence, and this is as much freedom as any reasonable ideal of liberty demands. Thus, a drug that gives people pleasure but reduces their freedom would be prohibited by the triple-barreled principle (apart from, say, special medical uses); a social program that makes a multitude happy but is unfair to a minority would be rejected as unjust. Moreover, although one may voluntarily devote one's life to enhancing the happiness (if only by reducing the suffering) of humanity, this is not obligatory. Thus, coercive force may not be used to produce such beneficence.[18]

A subsidiary principle is that moral virtue, understood partly as a disposition to act on the fundamental principle, should be taught, by example and precept. Some of the merits of the virtue tradition could thus be preserved, together with the utilitarian drive to make life better and the Kantian insistence that persons be treated as free and equal—a standard of conduct central for treating them as ends. Treating them as ends requires respecting their freedom; acting on rationally universalizable principles requires obeying rules under which basic equality is respected (or those in the disadvantaged position could not accept them.) Moreover, intuitive moral principles of the kind articulated by Ross can be taken to be in some way derivable from the fundamental principle.[19] Even apart from that, they express standards of conduct essential in understanding the practical applications of that principle.

A Contractarian Approach

One other framework for deriving moral standards should be considered in this section: contractarianism. The broad idea underlying this approach in ethics is that when a moral principle can be derived from a hypothetical contract that meets certain conditions, it may be considered to be justified. Early uses of contractarian thinking include Thomas Hobbes, John Locke, and Jean-Jacques Rousseau.[20] The leading contemporary version of the view is that of John Rawls, who uses a contractarian framework as partial justification of two principles of justice.

On Rawls's view, we imagine rational persons deciding, from behind a "veil of ignorance," on what principles of justice to live by (the veil is required to prevent those choosing from being biased in their own favor—say, prejudiced by believing that they will be unusually high in intelligence or health needs). He argues that they would choose the following: first, a principle of liberty, on which "each person is to have an equal right to the most extensive basic liberty compatible with a similar liberty for others"; second, a principle determining justly allowable differences: "Social and economic inequalities are to be arranged so that they are both (a) reasonably expected to be to everyone's advantage and (b) attached to positions and offices open to all" under conditions of equal opportunity.[21]

The contractarian approach to justifying moral principles is, in a certain sense, not basic: one must at least build in assumptions about what counts as rationality and what values are to be preserved by the contract. For Rawls, "The concept of rationality invoked here, with one special assumption, is the standard one familiar in social theory. . . . A rational person . . . follows the plan which will satisfy more of his desires rather than less and which has the greater chance of being executed" (p. 143), where the special assumption is that "a rational individual does not suffer from envy" (p. 143). As to the value assumptions, he takes "primary goods" to provide substantive standards for decision behind the veil of ignorance. These include "rights and liberties,, powers and opportunities, income and wealth . . . self respect" (p. 62).[22]

Whether or not one accepts Rawls's principles of justice in particular, one can use a contractarian framework similar to his to provide some justification for various kinds of moral principles, including the pluralist universalism suggested earlier. Doing this is a major task; but it should be obvious that it can be executed in a way that supports the various intuitively plausible moral principles I am proposing—the Rossian principles together with the pluralist universalism that serves as at least a partial summary of its requirements.

The Decision Problem

Given the richness of all these ethical approaches and the principles common to them, how, in practice, are we to decide what we (morally) should do? It would be unrealistic to claim that any good ethical approach makes this easy in all cases. But suppose we understand our most general principles—whether double-barreled, as Kant's intrinsic end formula is, or triple-barreled, as the suggested pluralist universalism is—in light of the commonsensical principles Ross articulated, which are supported by virtually all the major ethical theories and (in part for that reason) will be the concrete standards I will most often treat as a starting point for ethical reflection. If Rossian principles are taken as a major starting point in ethics, it is often quite clear what we ought to do.

The idea of taking the common-sense Rossian intuitive principles as a starting point in ethics may seem to presuppose more consensus than there is in moral matters. That is arguable, but I believe that there is among the great moral philosophers and other ethical theorists a considerable agreement on what sorts of things we should and should not do: we are, for instance, not to kill, lie, or enslave; we are to keep promises, help to relieve suffering, develop our capacities. Some of the crucial standards, moreover, are reflected in modern legal documents, such as the U.S. Constitution, especially the Bill of Rights, which emphasizes freedom and implicitly affirms many kinds of obligation of non-injury. Famously, the First Amendment affirms both separation of church and state and religious liberty (both values to be discussed in chapter 4): "Congress shall make no law regarding an establishment of religion, or prohibiting the free exercise thereof . . ." (Amendments, Article 1, passed by Congress September 25, 1789).

3. Ethics and Science: Beyond the Stereotypes

Ethics and science are often considered so different as to have little in common. But despite their significant differences, there is an important similarity. Just as scientists give different theories to account for the same experimental data, moral philosophers propose different principles of ethics to account for the various—and usually plausible—common-sense moral judgments they share. The idea is in part this. We may view scientific inquiry as aiming at an account of perceptual (roughly observational) experience and of the apparent truths our experience reveals, for instance general truths about the observable behavior of plants and animals, of gases and metals, of people and their creations. Analogously, we may regard ethical inquiry as aiming at an account of our moral experience and of the apparent truths it reveals, for instance intuitively clear truths about the terrible experience of being oppressed, which we judge to be *unjust*, about the richly welcome experience of being cared for when we are sick, which we judge to be *good*, and about the reassuring or, sometimes, satisfying experience of receiving an apology, which we judge to be *owed* to us. The idea that justice requires a kind of equal treatment of persons and the idea that restrictions of human freedom are justified only for self-defense or protection of the innocent explain the intuitions regarding the wrongness of oppressive acts (though these ideas are not the only possible explanations).

Rational Disagreement

Moreover, just as there is moral disagreement, there is scientific disagreement. But at least most moral disagreement disappears when the parties to the dispute are liberated from confusions and come to agree on all the relevant (non-moral) *facts*.[23] Moral disagreement in complex matters is one place in which scientific investigation can be crucial for the practical application of ethics. Consider capital punishment. Does it deter better than long-term incarceration? Does it adversely affect those who must administer it? Perhaps only careful scientific inquiry can tell us.

To be sure, capital punishment *may* be an exception to the thesis that an adequate grasp of the relevant facts tends, when the facts are analyzed without confusion, to produce moral agreement. But certainly factual disagreement on its effects is a major element in the dispute.[24] So is logic: poor reasoning even from all the relevant facts may account for disagreements that morally divide people who would otherwise agree. But there may also be analogous cases in which scientists agree on the experimental data in a given domain and differ in the theories they take to explain the data.[25] Science should not be represented as a realm in which consensus is universal—or even always possible.

Three Kinds of Moral Centering

Whether we combine the great one-factor ethical theories or not, we learn something from all three kinds. Let me briefly summarize some of it in relation to the idea that an ethical view can provide a central focus for raising and, if only gradually, answering moral questions.

Virtue theories tell us to concentrate on developing virtuous character and, in that sense, on *being good*. For them, the fundamental question of ethics is, What is it to be a virtuous person? Above all, what are the virtues (excellences) of character, and—on the practical side—how should we cultivate them? These will include justice, honesty, and beneficence, but overall excellence of character will exhibit not only other virtues but also an integration among them all that enables us to act morally. For Aristotelian virtue theories, virtue is a kind of activity concept, and the question of what it is to be virtuous is inseparable from the question of how one should live.

Kantian and intuitionist theories (the kind called *deonto-logical*, meaning roughly 'duty-based') tell us to concentrate on the *quality of our acts*—their justice or injustice, benefi-cence or harmfulness, truthfulness or deceitfulness, and so on. For them, the fundamental question of ethics is, What kinds of acts—understood in terms of appropriate principles of action—are intrinsically appropriate for us as, above all, free beings with dignity?[26] They will include abstaining from the kinds of abusive and deceitful acts that tend toward treat-ment of people merely as means, but they will also include end-regarding acts such as promoting people's happiness and enhancing their liberties—the kinds of acts that are char-acteristically instances of treating others as ends.

Utilitarian theories (the main kind called *teleological*, mean-ing roughly 'result-oriented') tell us to *produce as much good*—most important, happiness—as we can. For them, the funda-mental question of ethics is, What kinds of acts have the best consequences? These theories are thus *consequentialist*, a broader term than 'utilitarian' that can be used for views that call for promoting not human happiness but, say, satisfaction of basic desires. Utilitarianism is the most familiar kind of con-sequentialism and asks, What kinds of acts tend to *maximize* human happiness? (In some versions the pleasure and pain of animals is also considered.) Here relief of suffering is as im-portant as production of happiness; psychological as well as physical well-being is included; and, insofar as (e.g.) honesty and justice contribute to happiness in the broad sense, the acts necessary for achieving honesty and justice are also required.

These three kinds of ethical view give us, then, a charac-ter standard (virtue theory), a personal, qualitative conduct standard (Kantianism and intuitionism), and an impersonal, quantitative conduct standard (utilitarianism). And pluralist universalism stresses all three variables: kind of action, overall consequences for happiness, and character.[27] It is morally important what kind of action we perform quite apart from its consequences, but the consequences of what we do are also morally important; and without good character we cannot be counted on do the right things, bring about good consequences by our acts, or act for the kinds of reasons we can be proud to acknowledge to others. These differing theories may be compared to differing scientific theories of a given kind of phenomenon, such as the nature of light. They can agree about certain moral principles, such as the intuitive common-sense moral principles calling for honesty, beneficence, and non-injury, even if, like different theories of light, they explain differently why the principles hold.

4. Relativism and Objectivity

So far, I have sketched a diverse range of positions in ethics. These significantly overlap. The diversity they represent may not preclude a kind of unifying picture of the place of morality in human life. That diversity may also be consistent with a set of basic principles and basic values that virtually any rational person can accept. Diversity need not lead to fragmentation. The characters, subplots, and scenes in Tolstoy's *War and Peace* are highly diverse, but the novel is not fragmentary. Fragmentation does, however, beset many contemporary discussions of ethics. Some of the fragmentation is theoretical— a result of different people's adhering to conflicting abstract standards for evaluating action, say a secular welfare standard and a theologically based vision of life. Some of it is a matter of disagreements concerning specific issues, such as legalization of assisted suicide or of certain drugs. This book aims in part to provide an understanding of both kinds of fragmentation—in theory and in application—and to develop a perspective that helps to overcome it. I want to begin with a major source of theoretical fragmentation.

Two Types of Relativism

We hear a great deal about the relativism of our age. But what is relativism? Clearly, what one ought to do depends on, and is in *that* sense relative to, circumstances. Normally, we ought not to slap people; but if someone groggy from sleeping pills must wake up or die, we may then be obligated to slap quite briskly. We could call this view *circumstantial relativism* (circumstantialism for short): it says that what we ought to do depends on, and so varies with, and must be *relativized* to, the relevant circumstances.

Circumstantial relativism is not highly controversial. But suppose someone said that the principle which I have just shown to apply differently in two different situations—the principle that one ought not to slap people—is *itself* relative, in the sense that its "validity," roughly its justifiability as a principle of prima facie obligation, depends on the society (or culture) in which it is accepted. On this relativism, if our society does not endorse the principle that one should *not* slap people or the principle that one *should* make an effort to help injured people, then we have no obligation to abide by these principles. Call this view *status relativism*: it says that the *justifiability*—the validity status—of moral principles is relative, for instance relative to custom, and that ethics therefore has no universally justifiable binding principles.

Circumstantial relativism says that the *application* and interpretation of moral principles varies with circumstances—and so, despite the moral prohibition on slapping people, you may slap someone whose life depends on it. Status relativism says that the *justification* of moral principles depends on circumstances and is not objective, so it is only a matter of, say, what is prevalent in your society, whether you have any obligation not to slap people or to save their lives. By contrast—status relativists tend to grant—science and mathematics *do* have universally justified principles that are *not* relative to what prevails in a particular culture.

I believe that circumstantialism is sound and that status relativism is mistaken. The former is not usually controversial; the latter is often affirmed but rarely taken to its logical conclusion. It implies that there is no universally valid justification for believing that it is wrong to torture little children, that the Nazis did wrong in massacring Jews, and that lynching black teenagers for looking at white women is grossly unjust. These implications are indefensible.

Tolerance

There is far more to say about relativism, but the overall perspective I am developing is intended to emerge as a clearly preferable alternative. Still, one point is immediately evident: we do not need status relativism to account for *tolerance* as a valid ideal. Once that is fully appreciated, there is much less to motivate status relativism. Relativity of conduct to circumstances goes a long way toward grounding tolerance of different ways of doing things under different personal, social, and cultural circumstances. Indeed, tolerance itself is *best* supported by the view that there is a *universally* valid principle of tolerance, to the effect that people should be allowed as much freedom as *all* of us can have without harming others.[28] This is part of what I mean by freedom within the limits of justice.

There is widespread confusion about relativism and other views concerning the foundations of morality. Not only do many people tend to think that circumstantial relativity implies status relativity; many also think that objectivity in ethics would license an intolerant absolutism. That is a mistake. Again, it is helpful to compare ethics and science.

Science is objective, above all in resting on intersubjective methods of inquiry, the kind that any competent investigator can use; yet science is also *fallibilist*; its standards and methods presuppose the possibility of error. It is not absolutist, claiming certainty for its conclusions. It develops degrees of evidence for its hypotheses and theories, but it does not pretend to prove them absolutely or in a way that prevents rational doubt.

It should be granted that ethics is not quantitative, as natural science is. We cannot measure obligation as we can length. But quantification is not required for objectivity, as the case of the social sciences shows. They can achieve explanation and a good measure of predictive power even using psychological and social concepts, such as belief, desire, and value, that do not admit strictly quantitative measurement.[29] Indeed, even pure logic, as objective a discipline as there is, is not quantitative. It is *formal*, but not quantitative.[30]

Objectivity, Individuality, and Cultural Identity

If ethics is objective, how can it do justice to human happiness, which is subjective? What makes me happy may not make you happy, and one culture's favorite pastime may repel another: think of bullfighting, for instance. The important point here is that the view that happiness is good does not restrict it to any one *kind*: Aristotle and Mill, for instance, realized that there are as many kinds of happiness as there are activities that make people happy. In this way, happiness is a *multicultural* value.

Happiness, then, is an *objective* good—roughly, an actual good rather than one simply believed to be a good—but it is *subjectively* realized: it exists only *in* one or another life experience. This point supports a plausible view: a pluralist objectivism. We *do* have a universal value here, human happiness, but people can realize this good in their own ways.[31] The pleasures some get from seeing bullfighting are real goods, but that does not imply that these goods are or should be realizable in *my* experience. I would add that the pains suffered by the bull are also real—and one task of ethics is to help us weigh what is good against what is bad.

Are we now headed for chaos, allowing all to pursue happiness in their own way (with only the restrictions imposed by the prohibition of injustice and curtailment of liberty)?[32] No. For one thing, we are enough alike to have overlapping pleasures: normally, virtually all of us enjoy (to some extent) good food, social activity, the arts, sports, and other cooperative endeavors. We are even more alike in what makes us suffer—and in my view, reducing suffering generally has higher priority than enhancing happiness.

Suppose, as Mill argued, that some kinds of happiness are better than others. In this case the pursuit of happiness can be organized by priorities. For instance, people who have experienced both the pleasures of playing Beethoven's sonatas and those of playing Chopsticks generally prefer the former. To be sure, Mozart gave us the memorable melody of "Twinkle, Twinkle, Little Star," and the simple can be incomparably beautiful. But even this little gem is enhanced by variations. The question of qualities of happiness is difficult and important, and I will say more about it later.

5. Ten Challenges for Contemporary Ethics

If I have been right, there is fragmentation in ethics as a result of theoretical disagreements about the status of moral principles. There are tensions among status relativists on one side and objectivists on another, and there are many people who are confused about these and other matters. Some people in any of these categories can be easy victims of plausible demagogues or persuasive fanatics. A related source of fragmentation is the complexity and divisiveness of some of the major ethical challenges of contemporary life. These are too numerous to address in detail, but let me sketch some of them. I will keep them in view in the next two chapters but reserve for the last chapter a series of proposals for approaching them.

First, there is the *religion-politics problem*. This is the battery of questions concerning the proper limits of government policy as affecting religion. This problem besets any free democracy in which religion is a significant element, and it is specially acute for societies in which clergy have great power in government, as in certain Islamic countries. For simplicity, however, I will often focus on the United States, in which the Free Exercise clause in the Constitution (quoted above) has high authority. How much can the state do to accommodate religion without moving toward favoring one religion in particular (a significant danger where there is a majority religion)? May it, for instance, provide vouchers to pay for religious children to attend private schools? If, even without intending it, the state favors one religion over another, or even favors religion as opposed to secularity, does this tend to establish a religion? And how may a state protect, say, children's rights without impeding the free exercise of *someone's* religion, as when a judge orders a transfusion to save the life of a child of Jehovah's Witnesses, whose religion prohibits transfusions? I think we need a significant measure of separation of church and state. But what measure? On what principles?

The second problem I will address is very closely related to the first. Call it *the religious sensibilities problem*. This is a problem not for law but for individual conscience. It would persist even if we had a perfect relation between church and state at the institutional level. Suppose I disapprove of assisted suicide and the cloning of human beings because I think that God has given us a natural way of dying and of reproducing, and that any other way is irreverent and immoral. Is this belief an ethically sufficient basis for trying to dissuade secular scientific colleagues from trying to clone human beings or from even supporting this dramatic procedure? More important, is it an ethically sufficient basis for *illegalizing* such cloning? Similar kinds of questions occur concerning the legality of abortion.

The third challenge I will stress is exemplified not only by cloning but also by numerous other technological possibilities, such as those that facilitate the invasion of privacy. This challenge is *the gap between ethics and technology*—probably a widening gap. Among the most salient marks of advanced democracies is technological momentum. Technology is driven not just by the ubiquitous profit motive, but by our natural tendency to want to do things that are novel, striking, glamorous, or dramatic. This tendency may be indispensable to creativity and is often admirable. But as we have seen with cloning, technology sometimes proceeds so quickly that the ethical questions it raises are not anticipated. Here we need greater moral imagination and an application of sound moral standards to technological advances. One way to put the issue is this: Should technology be on a leash and, if so, how long a leash?

The fourth problem is perhaps the greatest tragedy of the developed nations: the tendency for the body to outlive the mind, which may severely atrophy while modern medicine preserves the body. It might be called *the problem of the moribund mind in the living body*. It is all too prominent in our nursing homes, and a great challenge to both our sense of duty toward the elderly and our ethical standards governing scarce resources. Much too commonly, mind death precedes brain death. We sometimes do too much to keep the body alive; we often pay too little attention to the mind. Or is the main need, as some think, drugs that prevent mental decay?

The fifth problem is a kind one might expect in certain societies with widespread prosperity. It is *self-indulgence*. In the individual, it is egocentrism—me-centeredness. Its social counterpart is the excessive concern with one's own circle—or nation, or religious group, or tribe—pretty much regardless of what happens to outsiders. Typically, this self-indulgence is combined with little or no resolve to achieve excellence, and it may contribute to the widespread cheating—in and outside education—that is disturbingly common.[33] Indifference toward the environment or animals or future generations is part of this problem; languishing on drugs is another. For the self-centered, others are important not in themselves, but mainly as means to an end. How can a free society—whose cultural coercion of ordinary citizens is usually limited to requiring a minimal education—create the incentives needed to combat this corrosive pattern? It is widely known that in the past decade America has seen increasing needs for people with advanced technical training to come from abroad and, correspondingly, an increasing number of foreign graduate students in mathematics and natural science.

The sixth problem is related to the fifth but is more a matter of national policies than of individual tendencies: it is *insularity*—the opposite of cosmopolitanism. In the individual, it is ignorance of other times, other places, other ways, and other cultures. This insularity is often reflected in institutions and the social fabric. At its worst, it breeds not merely a neglect of what is different, but a self-satisfied ethnocentrism. A primitive form of this excessive centering on one's own ethnicity or in-group is *tribalism*. Again, the problem is particularly serious for free and prosperous societies: how much education in the ways of other cultures should we require, and how much sharing with other societies, particularly those with widespread poverty, should we build into national policy—and taxation?

The seventh case is the *role model problem*, one that is particularly acute from the point of view of virtue ethics. Much of the world suffers from an insufficiency of good role models: there are either too few people exhibiting excellence, particularly excellence of character, or too few with enough influence relative to the ubiquitous bad role models, the heroes of violence and exploitation, power and ostentation, bigotry and xenophobia. Even those who confidently vote for political candidates are often disappointed by their character. Famous entertainers commonly lead lives of extravagance or, often, lives marked by infidelity or legal proceedings. The image of sports has often been tarnished by steroids and other violations.

Closely connected with the role model problem is *the media problem.* It is manifested especially in dumbed-down, sensationalistic, and stereotypic programming. Our broadcast and print media, now enhanced by the Internet, are a great opportunity for education and enrichment. But they are also a venue for glamorizing violence and sexual exploits. And the visual media in particular, whether in broadcasts or simply available on Internet sites, easily favor one-liners over careful analysis, and the striking image over the balanced description. One line can tell a lot, and striking images can spur worthy actions. But images can be powerfully manipulative, and a one-liner can supplant reasoning we sorely need. We cannot, however, solve the problem by legislating detailed standards; a free society must use the power of judgment, especially ethical judgment, to achieve social change without undermining liberty.

If we widen our perspective from any one society to international relations, we quickly find another (ninth) challenge: the *globalization problem,* particularly as related to social justice. One challenge is how the developed nations can do more to relieve suffering and overcome ignorance. But we must also prevent atrocities and other disasters, such as the commodification of children, the sexual slavery of women, and the continuing spread of AIDS in Africa and elsewhere. The world is getting smaller and more interconnected; the have-nots are increasingly aware of what the haves have.

This growing awareness can help to bring down tyrannical regimes, but it can also undermine democracy and spawn terrorism.

The tenth and final problem I will address is crucial for all the others. It is the *low level of discourse*. This is an ethical challenge both because good ethics in a complex world depends on clear communication and because a free society must state a cogent rationale for standards that burden its citizens, as do privacy incursions rationalized as protections from terrorism. The problem is not just poor literacy, but also its mathematical counterpart—*innumeracy*. We should be especially concerned about poor reasoning and uncritical habits of mind. Too few people can speak or even read at a high level; too few understand ratios, probabilities, and elementary statistics. An example of conceptual laxity, which also illustrates the dumbed-down-media problem, is the uproar that began early in 1992 about members of Congress supposedly writing bad checks. Repeatedly we heard of checks "bouncing," but (to my knowledge) few if any of the checks were returned for insufficient funds. Rather, our representatives helped themselves to interest-free loans. This *is* unethical—and self-indulgent. But my main point is that one senior journalist after another—and most members of Congress—let the inaccurate and morally worse description of the conduct go uncorrected.

This is a time of powerful challenges to ethics, both theoretical and practical. Ethical views are widely misunderstood, frequently mistrusted, and often thought to be, in comparison with scientific theories, subjective or valid only relative to a culture. Quite apart from the difficulties facing ethical theory, there are numerous contemporary problems that challenge our ethical thinking. These include problems centering on religion and citizenship, on rapidly advancing technology, on the extension of human life beyond our years of vitality, on selfish preoccupation with one's own pursuits at the expense of the environment and the future of humanity, and on the intellectual quality of our discourse, the very fabric of our communal lives.

On the positive side, I have also described major ethical views that, developed separately or in combination, offer guidance; and in the very recognition of the theoretical and practical problems I have described, we can begin to work toward resolutions. A good resolution must be guided by values. Are there major life-orienting values that we can share? Can they be connected with sound moral principles in a way that enables us to agree on how to approach our major problems? Can we nurture tolerance without indiscriminately blessing whatever anyone earnestly wants to do? How can we combine tolerance for diversity with standards of excellence? Some of these questions of value are perennial, but they are particularly urgent now. Questions like these and the moral values and ideals we can rely on in dealing with them will be the main concern of chapter 2.

2

THE EXPERIENCE OF VALUE

What Do We Value, and Why Should We Care?

Chapter 1 described two kinds of challenges to ethics. There are theoretical challenges that threaten to undermine the authority of moral standards, and there are practical challenges that can be met only by standards of morality and value that earn conviction and inspire conduct. I sketched some major kinds of moral view: virtue ethics and several rule views—divine command, Kantianism, utilitarianism, intuitionism, and a pluralist universalism that integrates elements from all of these. Pluralist universalism takes justice, freedom, and happiness to be the central standards in ethics, and it takes intuitive common-sense moral principles to be a good indication of the day-to-day standards we should abide by under those three kinds of theory.

All of the major ethical views either take some notion of value—such as the intrinsically good—to be central for morality or at least give an important place to value. For utilitarianism, value, understood in terms of pleasure and pain broadly conceived, is central, but every plausible ethics gives these notions an important place. Moreover, the most plausible ethical views distinguish between what we must do to avoid wrongdoing and, on the other hand, what is *supererogatory*: good or in some way praiseworthy, but going beyond the call of duty.[1]

Value, then, plays at least two guiding roles. First, what is valuable, for instance liberty and justice, provides a set of restraints. It must be in some way *protected* by moral conduct and so limits what we may do. Second, the realm of the valuable contains a set of ideals and thereby directs our best energies, say in art and science. Our corresponding values—our valuational attitudes—express our *aspirations* and thereby challenge us to see what we *can* do; and they determine *constraints*, and thereby limit what we *may* do.

1. Value versus Valuation

One more point is essential before we explore value. I have been referring to the valuable in the sense of what is good in itself. This is commonly called *intrinsically good* or, in another common terminology, intrinsically desirable. What is intrinsically good is contrasted with what is instrumentally good: good, or desirable, *as a means*—as an instrument, if you like—for bringing about something else.

Something can be *both* intrinsically and instrumentally valuable. Enjoying beautiful music can be both good in itself, since there is goodness in the experience itself, *and* also a means to relaxation, since the enjoyable experience can produce relaxation. But instrumental goodness is relative and need not provide any reason for action to realize it. The instrumental goodness of a weed killer for destroying a flower bed does not give us a reason to use it thus; and if the weeds it is designed to kill cease to be a problem, we may discard it.[2] By contrast, the intrinsic goodness of enjoying beautiful music provides us with a reason to seek such experience. We are not in general able to realize all the kinds of intrinsic goods, but something intrinsically good is never to be cast aside like an obsolete instrument.[3]

There are not only things that are intrinsically good, but also things that are intrinsically bad, intrinsically undesirable (*disvaluable*). There is probably more agreement about what is intrinsically bad than about what is intrinsically good. If nearly everyone takes enjoying something (at least something not hurtful to others) to be intrinsically good, even more take pain and suffering to be intrinsically bad. The bad sets important negative standards, such as avoiding the causing of pain. It also shapes those positive goals that are defined in relation to the bad: for instance, the goal of eliminating, as opposed to simply not causing, fear, disease, and starvation.

It may well be, as some philosophers hold, that the moral importance of abstaining from doing evil is—other things being equal—greater than that of promoting good.[4] When other things are equal, *reducing* evils that exist is apparently a more important moral aim than positively promoting the good. I presuppose this in discussing moral issues, but little I will say depends on it. Moreover, my concern ranges beyond moral requirements to the general subject of value, including many kinds of non-moral value, such as the goodness of art.

It is easy to fall into confusion in thinking about value. For one thing, it is easy to miss the distinction between intrinsic and instrumental value. A good diet is so important that it might easily be considered intrinsically valuable, as indeed the pleasures of consuming it may be. Money can so readily lead to things good in themselves that it may be taken to have value in itself. Important goods, then, may still be instrumental. Moreover, as a good diet shows, even when things we do *lead* to something good in itself, as eating well may lead to enjoying good health, they may or may not be *accompanied* by intrinsic goods, such as the pleasures of eating delectable foods.

A second distinction is no less important. Given how often we speak of people's *valuing* this or that, and of "human values," a different confusion easily arises. *Value* as a kind of worth is one thing; valu*ing*, as something close to caring about, is another. Mixing these up is abetted by how commonly what we care about *is* intrinsically valuable and hence *has* non-instrumental worth—value even apart from any good effects. Valuing the valuable is fitting; but, as vanity and hunger for power show, people sometimes care about things that are neither good in themselves nor lead to anything that is. Valuing is not always directed toward the valuable.

The notion of the intrinsically *valuable* is normative and belongs to ethics and fields that provide prescriptive standards: roughly, standards indicating what we should do. The notion of *valuing* is psychological and is descriptive rather than prescriptive. Valuing is at least threefold. To value something is (roughly) to want to experience, possess, or bring it about; to tend to feel positively toward it; and, in those who have value concepts, to tend to believe it to be (in some way) valuable. We value some things, such as good conversation, intrinsically; others, such as insurance policies, we value instrumentally, as *means* to something further. Both intrinsic and instrumental value are (in different ways) threefold in the way just described. But unfortunately we can value, in either way, what is *not* good in any sense. We can also fail to value what *is* intrinsically good. We educate the sensibilities, morally, aesthetically, and in other ways to prevent this regarding the intrinsically good (which is the kind of value of concern here). If we fail in educating them, ethics cannot get a good grip. This is one reason why, in examining contemporary ethical challenges, we must consider value.

2. The Good and the True

It should help in understanding and tracking the relation between valuing and value to compare it with the relation between believing and truth. Valuing is to value much as believing is to truth.

Truth is in a way the standard for belief: if we believe what is true, then we are, at least in an objective sense, cognitively successful—successful from the point of view of what has commonly been called "theoretical reason." If we believe what is not true, we are in error. This is an objective cognitive failure.

Value—in the form of intrinsic goodness—is quite plausibly considered to be the standard for valuing in much the way that truth is the standard for believing: if we value, for its own sake, something that is intrinsically good, then we are, at least in an objective sense, successful from the point of view of practical reason, just as we are successful from the point of view of theoretical reason if we believe, in response to the evidence, what is true. If we value, for its own sake, what is not intrinsically good—money, domination, weapons—we are in error.[5] Adequately well-grounded valuing of the good is like adequately well-grounded believing of the true. Both are fitting to their respective grounds and desirable; but, unfortunately, well-grounded valuing of the good can be mimicked by valuing something bad, as well-grounded believing of the true can be mimicked by believing something false. Some bad things can have the appearance of goodness, as some falsehoods can have the appearance of truth.

Scientific inquiry and other kinds of intellectual investigation, say in mathematics or philosophy, can detect errors constituted by believing false propositions. It is controversial whether intellectual investigations can detect errors in valuing things—above all, in valuing experiences and actions. The kinds of inquiry appropriate for detecting and rectifying errors in matters of value are important in ethics. Let us explore some matters of value to see whether there are undeniably good and bad things in life that may help us to articulate standards of conduct and, perhaps, a related conception of excellence.

3. The Primacy of Experience

I have said that what is intrinsically good provides a reason for action. It may also be uncontroversial that whatever else is true of the intrinsically good, realizing it (to a sufficient extent) is what makes life worthwhile. A life with nothing good in it is not worth living. A thing that cannot contribute to the worthwhileness of a life is not a candidate to be an intrinsic good.[6] It is in experiences that the *basic* goods are realized. We can experience love and beauty, conversation and sports, artistic and religious expression. We can also experience hunger and disease, hard labor and crowded living conditions, war and its carnage. Experience is the raw material of life. It is what we must build on and enrich if life is to be worthwhile.

I have given examples of good and bad experiences, such as the enjoyment of good music and the suffering of intense pain. But are there not basic goods that are *non*-experiential, such as a poem or a painting? These are sometimes said to be intrinsically good, but they are not experiences. Consider this closely. If you consider certain poems intrinsically good, what is your aim toward them? It is, say, to read them. But reading them is an experience. To be sure, a good poem is, as such, not an instrumental good. This is because the poem is *essential* and not merely instrumental to—merely a means that leads to—the goodness of reading it. An instrumental good is one among other possible means to something else (characteristically, to something good in itself). But there is no other possible way ("means") to the good of enjoying a poem other than experiencing it, say by reading or hearing the poem. Still, the primary reason for valuing the poem lies not in the poem itself taken in isolation from readings of it, but in the *rewarding* reading of it. I suggest we call things that are good in this way *inherently good* and that we call the experiences to which they are essential *intrinsically good.*[7]

The main point can be put this way: it is by experience that we properly determine what is intrinsically good; this holds whether we say that it is certain experiences that are the primary bearers of intrinsic goodness or, instead, that such goodness is also possessed by the objects of those experiences.

Thus, if you like, you might call inherent goods *unrealized intrinsic goods* and intrinsic ones *realized intrinsic goods;* the former are, as it were, waiting to be realized in intrinsically good experiences.

If we recall the analogy between the (intrinsically) good and the true, a natural picture emerges. Just as, when we are functioning properly, our beliefs formed in perceptual experience—which, we trust, is of the real world—are rational and tend to be true, so when we are functioning properly, our valuations and desires formed in pleasurable or painful experience—which, we trust, is of the good and the bad—are rational and tend to be sound, that is, to be of something that really is good or bad.[8]

This analogy is not meant to imply that we can literally perceive value. But it does suggest that pleasure and pain are commonly responses to something in experience, and provide us with reasons to act, much as sensory percepts (such as color sensations) are responses to something in experience and provide us with reasons to believe. More broadly, just as, normally, the sensory qualities of experience apparently reveal truth to us, hedonic qualities of experiences (their pleasurable and painful qualities) normally reveal value to us. Pleasure and pain, however, despite their being as multifarious as these experiences, may not be the *only* experiential responses that bespeak value. We can see this by exploring some of the differing dimensions of value.

4. The Multiple Dimensions of Value

I have suggested that pleasure is intrinsically good and pain intrinsically bad. Historically, these have been the most common candidates for basic values. Who would deny the goodness of enjoying a cool swim on a blistering day or the badness of being burned? But what about sadism? Can pleasure in hurting someone be intrinsically good? We want to say no, because such pleasure must not be sought. Yet we may also say that the pleasure is a good thing *in* the lives of sadists, though taken in the wrong object; it might, after all, "make their day." But it is not good *overall* that anyone should have a good day of that kind.

Hedonic Value

On my view, sadistic pleasure, insofar as we can *isolate* it, is what we might call a *narrow* good, but is also a kind of good that, being painful to the person it victimizes, is one that a person should not have. Just as a beautiful painting that clashes with the wallpaper behind it can make an ugly spectacle, the whole state of affairs, the sadistic pleasure taken in hurting the victim, can be bad overall—indeed, morally revolting and an ugly spectacle in our experience. Still, if we deny that the pleasure is good in any sense, why do we dislike seeing a sadistic person have it even more than seeing a normal person who lapses into a sadistic moment have it? We also properly disapprove of people's enjoyment of administering cruel treatment even if we cannot stop it (say, because it is legally required punishment). Suppose, however, that the victim is masochistic and so enjoys being pained. It is now less difficult to see how the sadist's enjoyment of causing the pain is a good in that person's life. To be sure, we would still prefer (for reasons to be explained shortly) that the sadist not enjoy accommodating the victim.

It should be evident that to say that pleasure and pain are among the basic values—meaning good and bad things—is not to be specific. For pleasure and pain differ dramatically across the territories of experience that yield them. This is particularly so for pleasures, which I will consider more often than pain. The sadistic pleasure is not an overall good, even if it is taken in actions there is some reason to perform.

Aesthetic Value

In the aesthetic realm, think of natural beauty or of good painting, music, sculpture, and literature. Of these, it is only poetry that I can bring to life right here to illustrate. Here is Shelley's telling sonnet, "Ozymandias" (the Greek name of Ramses II, the Egyptian monarch who, in the thirteenth century B.C., had a huge stature of himself erected):

> I met a traveler from an antique land
> Who said: Two vast and trunkless legs of stone
> Stand in the desert . . . Near them, on the sand,
> Half sunk, a shattered visage lies, whose frown
> And wrinkled lip, and sneer of cold command,
> Tell that its sculptor well those passions read
> Which yet survive, stamped on these lifeless things,
> The hand that mocked them, and the heart that fed:
> And on the pedestal these words appear:
> "My name is Ozymandias, king of kings:
> Look on my works, ye mighty, and despair!"
> Nothing beside remains. Round the decay
> Of that colossal wreck, boundless and bare
> The lone and level sands stretch far away.[9]

Those last lines spread out in sound to evoke the lonely sands they depict. In both sound and sense they recall the desolation they describe. We can stop there, with that stark portrait; but we may also find here a poignant description of the ultimate emptiness of the king's temporal glory.

In one of Emily Dickinson's poetic sketches of life, we find our subject—value, with pleasure and pain conceived as central—poignantly recognized:

> The heart asks pleasure—first—
> And then—Excuse from Pain—
> And then, those little Anodynes
> That deaden suffering.

> And then—to go to sleep—
> And then—if it should be
> The will of its Inquisitor
> The privilege to die—[10]

Not only does she capture the centrality of pleasure and pain in the human odyssey; she also portrays death as, at a certain point, a privilege. There is significance for medical ethics here, too, but the aesthetic value of the poem goes far beyond its intellectual insight.

It may be evident that not all of the aesthetically good experiences I have portrayed are necessarily pleasurable. If there is pleasure in reading Shelley's sonnet, there is also something ominous about it; and Dickinson's "The Heart Asks Pleasure–First–" is almost painfully melancholy. Consider also Macbeth's final, unmitigatedly bitter judgment of his misspent life. We cannot take unmixed pleasure in his scathing words:

> Tomorrow and tomorrow and tomorrow
> Creeps in this petty pace from day to day
> To the last syllable of recorded time.
> And all our yesterdays have lighted fools
> The way to dusty death. Out, out, brief candle!
> Life's but a walking shadow, a poor player
> That struts and frets his hour upon the stage and
> Then is heard no more. It is a tale told by
> An idiot, full of sound and fury, signifying nothing.

The value of aesthetic experience may always reside *partly* in pleasure, but pleasure is not its only element.[11] Indeed, Macbeth himself indicates the importance of non-hedonic values when he describes what is missing in his life. He laments:

> My life is fallen into the sere, the yellow leaf,
> And all the things that should accompany
> Old age—honor, pleasure, troops of friends—
> I must not look to have.

Here honor comes even before pleasure, and friendship is included as another good distinct from pleasure. To be sure, honor provides *retrospective pleasure* like nothing else. But its value is not just in the pleasure associated with it, and anyone for whom the value of friendship lies only in the pleasures it yields is missing part of its core.

Spiritual Values

In the spiritual and religious domains, too, there are experiences of intrinsic value. There is, for instance, the sense of being blessed, loved, connected with nature; the experience of beauty as something created, the joyous feeling of gratitude sometimes felt for life itself or for its deepest moments. Aesthetic experiences, both in nature and through responses to the arts, including the performing arts, are common sources of such experiences, but spiritual experience is not reducible to aesthetic experience or any other kind. It is often accompanied by a sense of meaningfulness in life; but that sense alone does not suffice for it.[12]

One might think that taking these experiences to be genuinely valuable presupposes the truth of theism. But even those who think that spiritual experiences, or certain of them, indicate the presence of God need not claim that, simply as valuable experiences, they logically require God's existence. Some spiritual experiences may be integrated with or even require faith, or at least a kindred kind of religious openness, but that is a different point. If there should be no God underlying such experiences, they would lack a kind of metaphysical basis; but, *as* experiences, they need be no less rich for that.

Value and Emotion

Love is another example of a value whose experience crosses dimensions, for instance the religious, the aesthetic, and the hedonic (the realm of pleasure and pain). Perhaps love has its irreducible emotional elements of value as well. There are distinctive ways of feeling that belong to love as felt toward the beloved. These are different in romantic relationships from what they are in familial ones or in friendships. They are sometimes as positive as the perfect attunement of one person to another in activities that give them joy; they can be as negative as the sight of a loved one pained and dying. They are a major source of the sense of meaning in life.

Hatred, by contrast, has disvalue across its many dimensions. It can be a kind of suffering and thereby hedonically bad, a kind of immorality and thereby ethically bad, and a kind of ugliness, and thereby aesthetically bad. It can embitter life. This is one reason why forgiveness, which eliminates hatred, is often so liberating. Forgiveness also has its own positive value. It can restore a good relationship, remove obstacles to fulfilling our capacities, and enhance our sense of an open future where we had been preoccupied with wrongs of the past.

The Realm of Sport

Particularly in America, but increasingly throughout the world, we must not neglect the athletic realm, conceived broadly enough to include any physical games. Athletic pleasures are an important kind, and they should not be taken to include only physical pleasures or those of winning. The sense of teamwork can have great positive value; winning is not the only athletic good. Sports can be blended with friendship as well as pursued to achieve the pleasures of improvement and mastery.

Athletic pleasures are particularly interesting because of how readily they are mingled with pain. Just as writers and other artists experience the pains of creation, athletes endure the pains of exertion. Given this blend of pleasure and pain, the overall value of an athletic experience may be difficult to assess. Running with an injured knee can be so excruciating as to be on balance bad even if one wins the race; but the pains of swimming the last lap may be a welcome sign of an unflagging speed that will set a new record. The aesthetic comes in as well: a tennis game can be elegant; the high jump-shot that is not even heard entering the basket can make a beautiful arc.

5. Moral Value

At this point you might easily wonder how moral value fits into the framework I have been building. Hedonists (such as Mill) must deny that there is *intrinsic* moral value. For them, moral value is simply an important kind of instrumental value. Actions and traits of character have moral value only insofar as they contribute in a certain way to happiness: to enhancing pleasure or reducing pain or both, i.e., to hedonic value. Thus, keeping a promise is not morally good as such; it is morally good insofar as it contributes to happiness (so some promise-keeping, by producing less happiness than breaking the promise, is not morally good). I agree that actions can have a kind of contributory moral value. But are not some positive and negative *intrinsic* values distinctively moral?

Consider, on the positive side, the sense of doing justice or of overcoming temptation to do something wrong. Doing justice, whether in designing a policy, in executing a will, or in determining a set of grades, can be very challenging. The sense of success here can be a reward of its own distinctive kind. On the negative side, think of the experience of being done an injustice or being cheated. Even if we suffer no pain from these—say, because we do not care about what is at stake—we may feel a special kind of resentment, revulsion, or violation that we dislike experiencing. It is unpleasant to have these and related experiences, but they need not cause pain or suffering. What is intrinsically bad in these (or some essential part of them) is not their unpleasantness but something like their moral repugnance.

Akin to this unpleasant experience of being done an injustice is that of being treated disrespectfully. This *can* be a kind of injury, but the distinctive damage is neither hedonic nor medical nor even emotional. By contrast, there is a welcome moral satisfaction in the contemplation of good character, especially in our friends and children, or of the kinds of good intentions Kant thought are crucial in good will.[13] Similarly, to uphold standards of honor against the blandishments of profit or the lure of self-advancement can be morally satisfying.

Moral values like these would be possible even where pleasure as such is absent. I say 'pleasure as such' because moral satisfactions share with pleasure a welcome positive quality; and in part for that reason they can contrast with pain and suffering somewhat as pleasure does. Indeed, moral satisfaction can counterbalance pain or suffering: its positive value can exceed their negative value. This can tempt one to assimilate moral satisfaction to pleasure or the value of such satisfaction to that of pleasure, but neither identification is warranted.

It is also easy to assimilate something else to pleasure: desire satisfaction, understood as the realization of *basic* desires. These are roughly desires directed toward things for their own sake, not toward things as means to something else that is desired. Such desires are most commonly for something, such as playing a game, *for* the anticipated pleasure. The frequency with which pleasure comes from satisfying basic desires leads to associating it with that. Still, some basic desires are not *for* pleasure, and not all pleasure is an effect or even accompaniment of desire satisfaction. We can want, for its own sake, to reduce or avoid pain; neither of these achievements need be pleasurable. Moreover, we could be neurologically or hypnotically manipulated to have basic desires for things from which we anticipate no pleasure, say for long walks in a chilling wind. The mere satisfaction of a basic desire need not, then, be pleasurable. We can also enjoy new things we had not wanted: unfamiliar tastes or sounds, the company of someone we dreaded meeting, a task we were talked into doing.

Equally important, because we can have basic desires for things whose realization is neither enjoyable nor worthwhile in any other way, desire satisfaction is not in itself intrinsically good or otherwise an ideal for human life.[14] Fortunately, much of what we naturally and basically desire, such as eating good food, having lively conversation, and playing games of skill, is such that satisfying the desires in question is intrinsically good. But what we desire cannot be the *basis* of what is intrinsically good; rather, a knowledge of what is intrinsically good can and should guide our desires.

6. The Organic Character of Value

Given our examples of good and bad things, there should be little doubt that there really are experiences which are intrinsically good and others which are intrinsically bad, and that each kind of experience provides reasons for action. There are positive reasons to bring about or preserve what is intrinsically good, and there are negative reasons to prevent or eliminate what is intrinsically bad. The reasons may not be conclusive. I may have reason to attend an enjoyable concert, but better reason to stay home. Even the second, better reason may not be conclusive: I may have a decisive reason to attend a graduation at the same time.

Some of our examples, for instance that of sadistic conduct, illustrate something more. They show that in matters of value the whole may be more (or less) than the sum of the values of the parts or aspects. Let me develop this point in both the moral and the aesthetic realms.

Consider the moral domain first. Suppose I am indignant about one person's wronging a weaker one. (Perhaps a boy forces his girlfriend to write his paper.) My experience of indignation is intrinsically unpleasant and, on that score, intrinsically bad.[15] But it is also fitting that I feel indignant at such exploitation. My reaction is morally fitting and, overall, can be intrinsically good. Here the moral goodness of the overall experience can outweigh its badness, which in this case is its intrinsic unpleasantness.[16]

A second example illustrates something that is at most implicit in the first: the non-additive, organic character of intrinsic value. As 'organic' suggests, there are biological analogues. Suppose we could keep all the parts of a person's body alive and assemble them in vats on a laboratory table. The totality of these parts, even if they remain alive, would not be a human being. And consider bridge cables. Working together, their hundreds of slender wires are vastly stronger than a single cable of the width of all of them put together. The principles of composition—or, often perhaps, the intuitions about composition—by which we determine the value of the whole from that of the parts are no doubt more straightforward in the case of the cable than with poems and paintings. But there is still a complex, and not merely additive, relation between the properties of the parts and those of the whole.

To see the moral application of organicity, imagine a hardened malicious murderer unrepentantly serving his sentence. A good thing, in his life, would be to enjoy television in the evenings in an easy chair. But would adding this good to his life produce a better overall state of affairs? Precisely because he is malicious and unrepentant, giving him a special pleasure is unbefitting to his punishment and would make the overall state of affairs in which he is central—namely, a malicious unrepentant murder's enjoying television in the evenings—worse than the state of affairs that existed before he was given television. If, however, intrinsic value were additive, then giving him the good thing constituted by the experience of television would *reduce* the overall badness of his unrepentant condition. As it is, adding such a good makes the resulting overall state of affairs worse: that a malicious murderer is unrepentantly serving his sentence *and* enjoying evenings in the way described is in itself worse than his simply unrepentantly serving that sentence.

By contrast, repentance, as a moral emotion appropriate to his crime, would be a good that makes the overall state of affairs constituted by his serving his sentence far better. His repentantly serving his sentence is a much better state of affairs than his unrepentantly doing so. This fact might well illustrate the organicity of value. The gain in value may well exceed the value of the repentance taken in isolation.

The repentance alone, however, may also illustrate the organicity of value. For suppose, as is not unlikely, that the discomfort, even painful distress, of his repentance constitutes a negative value that is quantitatively greater than the positive value of the sense of positive understanding of evil which is a requirement for genuine repentance. The total value of the repentance is still positive: even painful repentance can be positively valuable overall despite the negative value of the pain's "adding up to" a greater "quantity" of disvalue than the quantity of value in the (quite ordinary) understanding of evil that is a crucial element in the repentance. The pain *befits* the sense of evil in a way that enables the repentance to have a high degree of value.

The aesthetic realm provides similar examples. Consider the elements in a beautiful painting. Some that are aesthetically neutral in themselves can be indispensable to the beauty, hence to the aesthetic value, of the whole. Even a part of a painting ugly to view in itself can play an important part in making the whole artwork beautiful.

With poetry it is different: since each line must be taken in separately as well as placed in context of the whole, a bad line is very likely damaging. But in either aesthetic case, the value of the whole is not necessarily—and is in fact not usually—the sum of the values of the parts or aspects.

7. Fact and Value

If we treat intrinsic value as organic, and indeed as a special kind of property not accessible to ordinary scientific investigation, do we make it unacceptably mysterious? Surely not. To begin with, value is not the only thing that illustrates how the whole can be more than the sum of the parts. This is evident, as we have seen, from both biological and engineering analogues. I grant that (as noted in chapter 1), value is not "seen" or otherwise observable, as are some of the properties studied by science. Can anything be said to demystify value further? Two points should help.

The Objective Anchors of Value

First, though value is not itself a perceptual property (roughly, one accessible to the unaided senses), it is *grounded* in what is perceived or otherwise "objective." Its base is at least commonly in the natural world, even if value is not reducible to anything therein. The painting is beautiful—and so has aesthetic value—in virtue of its colors and shapes and certain relations among them, all of which are perceptible through the senses by ordinary observation. A deed is morally obligatory in virtue of being, say, the fulfillment of a promise, where an act of *promising* is observable in a quite ordinary sense that makes 'promise' a term appropriate for descriptive social science. These are properly viewed as genuine facts. They are simply not the same kinds of facts as those that ground them. There is no "fact-value gap" constituting a gulf between valuational facts and natural ones. There are simply different kinds of facts. Let us continue to explore how they are related.

Second, given the way value is grounded in what is objective, if two things or two deeds are exactly alike in their "descriptive" factual properties, such as those ascertainable by observation and scientific procedures, then they are also alike in intrinsic value. A perfect copy of a sculpture would have the same beauty as the original; a perfect replica of me would have the same psychological makeup, hence the same character, hence the same moral virtues (or vices).

Given this anchoring of values in descriptive properties, such as those characterizing the natural world, the values so anchored are subject to two kinds of requirements that are important both in ethics and in everyday appraisals of the good and the bad. One calls for consistency, the other for a kind of objective evidence.

The requirement of consistency is this: we must not ascribe different values or moral appraisals to things or deeds that are exactly alike, or even alike in just the relevant respects (this would seem to hold also for any religious or other "non-naturally" based values, such as pleasing God). This is why it is wrong to give different sentences to two teenage first-time offenders who share equally in a robbery and have entirely parallel pasts in regard to extenuating circumstances. They will differ in *some* ways, of course, but their color, height, tastes in music, and countless other characteristics are irrelevant to our moral appraisal of them.

Natural Facts as Evidences of Value

The second requirement concerns evidence for judgments of value. Since non-moral descriptive properties (a factual kind of property) are the ground of value, we should, with appropriate effort, be able to point to at least some such properties in justifying a value judgment or a moral assessment. To do this well takes great skill, but at least in ethics we have all the kinds of grounds moral philosophers have painstakingly described to use as a guide. A positive evaluation of an act that hurts the agent may be justified by noting that the agent *promised* to do it. This is to appeal to a fact relevant because it grounds a promissory obligation. A judgment that a person has done wrong can be supported by pointing to the person's fleeing an accident in which a child is thrown off a bicycle that skids on ice, where it was obvious to the fugitive that no one else could have helped. This appeals to a fact that grounds a second Rossian obligation, one of beneficence (which is here unfulfilled). Aesthetic judgments may also be justified by appeal to facts, though of course on different principles. A positive appraisal of a film, for instance, may be supported by the fact that large numbers of people who follow the cinema and are very different in character have enjoyed, avidly discussed, and emphatically praised the film.

Insofar as citing such descriptive factual grounds justifies moral and other normative judgments, these judgments are objective. And insofar as we can agree on what grounds are relevant, we can communicate the basis of our moral and other normative judgments. People differ in the abilities needed here. (To enhance these abilities is a major goal of a liberal education—perhaps of any sound comprehensive education.) Fortunately, we do tend to agree that lies and broken promises and injuries are in general wrong; that feeding the starving, healing the wounded, and preserving the environment are right and good; that enjoyable aesthetic experiences are to be sought; and that painful experiences of fire and ice are to be avoided. There is more clarity in some cases than in others, but every domain of value admits refinement of the sensibilities.

The great eighteenth-century philosopher David Hume expressed the components of this refinement in a memorable description of how artworks are to be judged. Of the "Standard of Taste," he said, "Strong sense, united to delicate sentiment, improved by practice, perfected by comparison, and cleared of all prejudice, can alone entitle critics to this valuable character," by which he meant, roughly, sound judgment; "the joint verdict of such," he continued, "is the true standard of taste and beauty."[17]

To be sure, we do not always agree on the quality of an artwork, any more than on the moral permissibility of a new research program. But given the intimate connection between moral and other value properties and their grounds in the natural world, we can agree on what is *relevant* to judgments of obligation and value even if we differ in certain overall appraisals.

This agreement on relevance is of major importance. Even when it is combined with disagreement in final judgment, agreement on what is relevant facilitates communication, negotiation, and reconciliation. I might particularly like the ominous ending of Shelley's "Ozymandias," and you might find it overdramatic, but we would agree on the importance of the dramatic element, and we could share a view on how to argue for our different assessments.

It should also be stressed that not all unresolved disagreement hinders the success of human relations. We can differ about the merits of two current plays and simply each go to a different one. And sometimes when it is not clear what option morality requires, that is because two or more options are equally good. Individual lives can vary both in the degrees to which they realize a given set of values and in their differing combinations of values. This is a welcome kind of pluralism.

———————

We now have the outline of a comprehensive moral view and a partial account of value. There are overarching standards of justice, liberty, and happiness; and there are everyday moral principles expressing obligations of honesty and fidelity to promises, of reparation and self-improvement, of gratitude and beneficence, and of justice and non-injury. There is also a multiplicity of values: moral, hedonic, aesthetic, spiritual, and religious. We should be constrained by moral standards and inspired by values. In both cases, there are standards we can share, and there are unlimited differences we may cultivate.

The principles and values I have described give us a framework for civilized life, but they do not make every moral decision easy. We still need to see how a life might be rationally structured in a way that yields *priorities* in matters of morality and value. Even an agreed list of moral principles and values does not tell us what combination of priorities is best for us. We must also seek an account of how to achieve those priorities that can be used by different kinds of people living in very different kinds of cultural circumstances and that can help us in meeting the ethical challenges described in chapter 1. That account is the main business of the next chapter.

PART II

HUMAN DIVERSITY AND THE ETHICAL CHALLENGES OF CONTEMPORARY LIFE

3

MORAL PLURALISM AND CULTURAL RELATIVITY

The first part of this book set out some of the major ethical standards that deserve reflection in the contemporary context. Chapter 1 sketches brief versions of virtue ethics and of Kantian, utilitarian, and Rossian intuitionist views. It also proposes, in outline, a pluralist universalism meant to capture the best elements in some of those major ethical theories. Chapter 2 explores the concept of intrinsic value and the domains of human life in which we can realize that value. I have argued that any sound ethical view must provide adequate standards in three different realms: first, justice in the distribution of the benefits and burdens of life; second, freedom of conduct; and third, welfare, in the broad sense of 'well-being', understood chiefly in relation to happiness on the positive side and suffering on the negative. This chapter will focus mainly on the kinds of lives we might lead if our ethical standards are basically of one or the other of the major kinds described in chapter 1 and our values incorporate the kinds of intrinsic goods portrayed in chapter 2.

1. The Diversity of Value

Meeting these or any other sound ethical standards requires fulfilling a multitude of specific obligations: obligations of veracity, beneficence, reparation, non-injury, and others. But the minimal fulfillment of obligation as understood in this pluralistic way—particularly for people who minimize their commitments to others—does not yield a good life for the agent. If, in fulfilling my moral obligations, I do only what morality strictly demands, my life is impoverished, and my contribution to the flourishing of others is quite limited.

To be sure, anyone who fulfills the demands of morality *for the right reasons*—a motivational achievement called for by all the great moral philosophers—is very unlikely to fulfill them only minimally. If I keep my word *from the virtue of fidelity*, make amends for my errors *with real repentance*, and do good deeds *from benevolence*, I will try to do as well as I can and will sometimes do supererogatory deeds. Even when what I do is a *minimal fulfillment* of obligation, I will not *merely fulfill* my obligation: I will do it from the kind of motivation that makes me morally creditworthy for my action.[1] This kind of moral conduct, as Kant saw, partly constitutes a morally good life.

Compare the disparity between thought and deed that Shakespeare describes so memorably in *Hamlet*. After his guilt drives him to attempt prayer, Claudius admits in his soliloquy:

> My words fly up, my thoughts remain below.
> Words without thoughts never to Heaven go. (Act 3, scene 3)

By contrast, if, in the right spirit, I do what morality requires, I will be manifesting my *values*; and, to some degree at least, those values will be *sound*, that is, their objects will really be *valuable*. Morally acceptable conduct that is *not* rooted in sound values tends to be in a way fortuitous. Rather as a lucky guess can sometimes hit the truth, the rightness of such conduct is good fortune, not the result of adhering to a sound guiding standard. Even morally acceptable conduct that results from a prudent determination to *seem* good does not reflect a stable pattern: people who are acting morally for appearances will often act otherwise when moral demands threaten their private projects. But sound values are important not only in providing a basis for moral conduct; they are also essential for a good life.

If the range of values I have described—including moral, hedonic, aesthetic, spiritual, and religious values—is representative, I think that this point will be obvious: a life without pleasure, or beauty, or social activities, or broadly spiritual rewards, or moral satisfaction is a kind that scarcely any thoughtful rational person would want to live. This is not to suggest a *formula* for a good life. I have argued that value is realized in experience, but not that any highly specific range of good experiences is required for a rewarding life. There is a plurality of good and bad things, and different good lives can realize and combine these diverse goods in many different ways.

Plurality, however, is not fragmentation, and pluralism is not "relativism." Why not, one may wonder, given how many different ways of living pluralism allows? Relativism, like so much else, comes in different kinds. Pluralism goes well with one plausible kind: circumstantialism, the view that what we ought to do in a given situation varies with, and is in *that* sense relative to, our circumstances. Neither view implies status relativism, the position that, even when circumstances are taken into account, the *justifiability* of moral principles is relative and hence there are no universal normative standards and the *validity* of moral judgments is relative to culture or circumstance.

That there are many kinds of goods, as pluralism affirms, does not entail that it is unimportant which goods one realizes or, especially, that whether to realize them at all, and whether some are superior to others, is not an objective matter. The good and the bad, like the right and the wrong, are grounded in facts about the world—including facts of human psychology—and both the good and the bad can be rationally appraised.[2]

Suppose you agree with what has so far been said about the plurality and objectivity of matters of morality and value. You might still doubt that there is anything beyond intuition or even a kind of personal taste to be appealed to in determining just how to structure one's life in relation to prioritizing certain values or certain moral demands on us. Since intuition and personal taste can be educated—for instance by experience, comparison, practice, and the elimination of prejudice, as Hume stressed in describing the "Standard of Taste"—it would not be a disaster for ethics if that doubt were warranted. But there is far more to be said about value and its role in guiding civilized life.

2. Human Sociality

Ethics is applicable mainly to interpersonal conduct, and the values we can realize in life require social relations. The major moral standards are realized chiefly in social contexts: right and wrong apply above all to our interpersonal conduct. It is true that value is realized in individual experiences, but this point is deceptive. For many of our best experiences are social or, if not strictly social, then socially grounded, as where we think of our audience as we write, or of the game we are to play as we practice alone.

Friendship and Love

There is also a connection between moral soundness and valuational success. Those whose lives do not include sound interpersonal values—valuations of intrinsically good things involving others—are less likely to be morally sensitive. Consider friendship. It is the kind of relationship that builds in those who share it such moral virtues as fidelity. Without these virtues it would be at best difficult to understand and fully respect others. Central to friendship are love and fidelity;

and in a good friendship there is pleasure in doing things together.

Love deserves special emphasis here. Loving others entails wanting their good for its own sake (hence intrinsically caring about it). And it is when we want the good of others for its own sake that we most easily and most effectively act morally toward them and, even in non-moral relations with them, take the greatest pleasure in their successes and joys. If we love our friends, we want them to enjoy life, and we want this *because* we value it for its own sake. Love for them does not make us want them to enjoy life because, for instance, they are better company when they are happy (though love does not rule that out as an independent reason for the desire). The goodness of their enjoyable experience is a good *reason* to value it and justifies that; valuing it is a good motivator of contributing to it and can *explain* our doing that; and contributing to the enjoyable experiences of others—providing company, resources, and support, for example—is a good way to do what is morally right in the relationship and can *constitute* both expressing the virtue of fidelity and fulfilling the obligation thereof.

Anyone who knows Kantian ethics should be reminded here of Kant's injunction (cited in chapter 1) that we must treat persons never merely as means, but also as ends. Friendship and love are a bulwark against treating persons merely as means, and they are *constituted* partly by attitudes that conduce to treating others as ends. If you are my friend, I must care about you *non*-instrumentally. Even benevolence, in the sense of goodwill toward you, is not enough, for I could want you to flourish *because* it will reflect well on me, as unfortunately some parents may want their children's success in order to live, or shine, through it. Instead, a measure of *altruism* is required for genuine friendship: I must want your good for *you*.

Ethical Prohibitions and Moral Freedom

This is an interesting place to observe the limits of even circumstantial relativity. Consider violence to persons, which is
generally wrong. Violence that is necessary for self-defense,
however, and is no more damaging than required for that
end, may be justified. If in certain circumstances an inherently bad thing can be justified, in other circumstances what
is generally good may fail to be desirable: beautiful music is
not an inherent good for the tone-deaf. But none of this implies that there are not objective limits on what can count as
the good of a person. Even if someone reflectively asks me
for a flogging, or to be my slave, I am not entitled to con-
clude that these things are for the person's good.[3]

The plurality of value allows that we may choose almost
without restriction what pleasures to pursue and what talents
to cultivate in order to realize one or another kind of good in
our activities; but it does not allow us to deny the value of
freedom, the badness of pain, or the moral wrongness of destroying normal human capacities. In a normal friendship,
none of this need even be said. Like unconsciously internalized grammatical rules that guide us without our even being
able to state them, these ethical constraints form part of our
framework of governing standards. But as with some of the
rules for clear expression, some standards of morality and
value should be articulated and discussed.

I have not meant to imply that without friendships in the
ordinary sense a person *cannot* be truly moral. Consider family relationships, and suppose (controversially) that these
need not be, even in a broad sense, cases of friendship. Family relationships normally embody the same kind of caring
for the good of the other for its own sake as do friendships.
That caring is indeed a defining property of parental affection. If family relationships are unhealthy—or, as may be

more common in the future, set aside in favor of upbringing by institutions or the state—can we reasonably expect the development of true morality? I doubt it, unless the institutional context is one in which there is something like parental affection or at least a climate favorable to developing friendship.

Many people hope that there will be increasing freedom from the burdens of child rearing. If this occurs, and, as we might expect, people become more wrapped up in their own pursuits, the needs and rights of children and the social support for morality will become ever greater concerns. It is in part because of children's needs and rights that cloning of human beings is objectionable. A cloned embryo would enter the world with only one "direct" biological parent. Even on the assumption that those who might allow production of a child from their genes will take responsibility for the child, the intimate relation to the "parent"—and the lack of any other parent—creates a situation presenting special and unpredictable ethical challenges. The problems will be different, and might be even worse, if artificial creation of adult persons becomes possible.[4] It is clear that, at least until these and other moral questions about cloning of persons are resolved, the artificial creation of persons goes beyond the ethically permissible uses of technology.

3. The Plurality of Integrated Lives

Let us suppose that the framework I have proposed is a good basis for understanding the demands of morality and the dimensions of value. And let us assume that we want to remain social beings. How should we try to structure a morally good life so that it is optimal in overall value—a life of genuine flourishing?

Virtues as the Fabric of Good Lives: Aristotle

For Aristotle, the good for human beings is flourishing, which in turn is achieved by our realizing the human virtues—the "excellences," as they are also called in some translations of Aristotle. (The word 'flourishing' is used for Aristotle's central term 'eudaimonia', which is also translated by 'happiness'.) There are many virtues, and virtues are to be *exercised,* not merely possessed. This is not the place to try to list all the virtues. My aim is just to sketch an Aristotelian integration of values as one ideal to serve as a guide in setting priorities. In doing this, I am not trying to do justice to the letter of his monumental *Nicomachean Ethics,* but only to its spirit.

The Aristotelian picture of the good life portrays a unity of the virtues under the guiding light of practical wisdom, wisdom in practical matters as opposed to theoretical ones such as those central in philosophy and mathematics, or physics and chemistry. Aristotle also posits a hierarchy in which some virtues are superior to others. In a famous passage, he calls *contemplation* activity characteristic of the highest virtue.[5] This is also given the high-brow translation 'philosophic contemplation' and the middle-brow translation 'study' (by W. D. Ross and Terence Irwin, respectively). In either case, we may need to remind ourselves how practical Aristotle was before we bristle too much from the aura of high-handed elitism. This is where we might concentrate on the spirit of his enterprise. Let us ask, then, how he distinguished higher from lower values and activities.

Perhaps his main principle of hierarchy is this: the highest excellence is the one proper to our most distinctive capacities.[6] He took these to be our rational capacities. We can agree that these operate at their best in intellectually demanding activities; but as much as I respect philosophical activity as demanding the use of reason, I cannot emphasize too much that the intellect functions in myriad other activities: scientific, aesthetic, religious, and indeed athletic (sports are not just physical exertions). If this is so, then given our different talents, some normal people might best achieve the highest excellence they can by concentrating on the intellectual and so pursuing a research field; but others might do better—even in using their rational capacities—by concentrating on excellence in, for instance, art, medicine, law, service, or (contrary to certain stereotypes) business. All of these require the use of reason and are fulfilled best when it operates at a high level. But suppose I have no aptitude for research fields. I may then be better able to use my rational capacities in a service profession in which my intellectual energies are focused on helping others.

How does pleasure come into the Aristotelian picture? For Aristotle, pleasure is not a sensation or even a psychological state of positive tone. It is, in the main sense, what he called a "supervening completion" of the successful exercise of human excellences: we take pleasure in doing *well* the things that express human excellence. We should *aim* not specifically at pleasure but at excellence in the activity in question, whether intellectual or artistic or social or athletic; but pleasure naturally comes with achieving excellence. Pleasures, then, come with flourishing; and the higher and more constant our realized virtue, the higher and more constant will be our pleasures.

Can anyone today live with this hierarchical, rather intellectualist Aristotelian picture? Some people can, as long as it is tempered by the pluralism that is in any case inevitable. The Aristotelian approach to ordering one's life does not dictate a rigid hierarchy. Indeed, to adopt a rigid hierarchy might bespeak failure to find, relative to our own character and capacities, a mean between excess and deficiency, as Aristotle's principle of the mean requires. Practical wisdom may be used—as it must be in any structuring of life's goals—in determining one's priorities. And what better principle for choosing a plan of life is there than one that bids us assess our talents in the light of our probable success in using our rational capacities in their exercise? For some, this means putting the things of the intellect first—philosophy or science or mathematics, for instance. For some, a life in social service may be the field of greatest flourishing. For still others, their talents best suit them for business, the arts, or sports.

Pleasure as the Basic Good: The Hedonism of Mill

If you recall the hedonistic notion of value central in Mill, you will find at least one contrast with the Aristotelian view of value. Aristotle's view does not make pleasure and pain central. Nor does it call for maximizing pleasure or minimizing pain. It *allows* us to maximize pleasure, but that is only because doing this can be compatible with or even a consequence of realizing our excellences. It also allows us to minimize pain, but this is mainly because doing so realizes an excellence (say in medical science) or because pain interferes with our realizing our capacities.

Mill knew Aristotle's ethical work, however, and he was attracted to the idea that the best ideal gives activities employing reason top priority. Mill's strategy for doing justice to the Aristotelian picture was to distinguish between higher and lower pleasures and to argue that the higher, qualitatively superior ones are those engaging our most complex faculties.[7] He took this into account in interpreting his call for maximizing the good. His actual test for hedonic superiority, however, is empirical and even lends itself to survey research:

> Some kinds of pleasure are more desirable and more [intrinsically] valuable than others. . . . Of two pleasures, if there be one to which all or almost all who have experience of both give a decided preference, irrespective of any

feeling of moral obligation to prefer it, that is the more desirable pleasure . . . the rule for measuring it [quality] against quantity, being the preference felt by [all or almost all?] those who in their opportunities of experience, to which must be added their habits of self-consciousness and self-observation, are best furnished with the means of comparison.[8]

This method of comparison and weighting is attractive to some people because it is *empirical*, in the sense (very roughly) that it proceeds by attention to what is indicated by observation or inference from what is observed, rather than just by reasoning about the matter. If you want to know whether enjoying Bach is better than enjoying rock or vice versa (or neither), start by learning to appreciate both and then see which pleasures—under the appropriate conditions—you prefer (you may prefer neither, since they could be equally desirable). Since you may not be representative, however, you must see how the comparison turns out for a fair sample of others as well.

Suppose Mill would have thought that the delightful contrapuntal variations in Bach would, in the special comparative circumstances he describes, appeal more than the less varied, often uniformly loud melodies of rock. Would he have to be heavy-handed or culturally imperialist here? Surely not. He would grant that some people do not have the ear for Bach and that some who do would, in some moods, enjoy far more (and hence could rationally prefer) the pleasures of hearing graphic lyrics belted out to rhythms that vibrate the very bones.

Mill's view calls for a democratic society that insists on education sufficient to enable people to make the needed comparisons—I suspect that nothing short of a good undergraduate education available to all will satisfy this criterion—but once we can sample the diverse pleasures of which we are capable,[9] we are free to pursue the life of pleasure in accordance with practical wisdom. That life is characteristically found through the preferences of "those who in their opportunities of experience, to which must be added their habits of self-consciousness and self-observation, are best furnished with the means of comparison." Whether this standard is sound or not, any plausible theory of the good life will need some appeal to practical wisdom. Mill is not alone in giving it a major role.

How does ethics fit into Mill's picture of the good life? Perhaps in part because he was influenced by Aristotle's case for the happy life, including friendship as an essential element in human flourishing, Mill took it that we can find much pleasure (and presumably pleasure of a high quality) in doing beneficent deeds. Here, as in comparing solitary with social pleasures, Mill was committed to being quantitative. We must all judge the pleasures of self-realization in comparison with those produced by service, such as bringing happiness to others; for *their* pleasure is as good as ours, and we must try to enhance it. We again find a significant role for practical wisdom in determining a plan of life.[10]

A Kantian Integration

If we turn to a broadly Kantian approach to unifying the quest for a good life, we find, as in other matters of obligation and value, a strong contrast with Mill and indeed with Aristotle as well. (By a broadly Kantian approach, I mean one that reflects major elements in Kant; it need not take account of all of his work, and my points will center on a reading of the theory of practical reason presented in his *Groundwork.*) Thus, good will must be taken as chief among the valuable things; Kant called it the only thing good without qualification,[11] and he took it to be above all directed toward doing the kinds of deeds required by the Categorical Imperative.

For a Kantian view, treating persons as ends, and avoiding treating them merely as means, will be essential for having good will and for living a good life. We are all ends, however—beings for whose sake positive things should be done and negative things avoided—and Kant took us to have obligations (duties) of self-improvement as well as obligations of beneficence. We are not, then, prevented from focusing our efforts on our own projects so long as we fulfill our other obligations. Moreover, non-moral value can be accommodated. We can realize it in our own lives, as when we pursue the arts and sciences; and we should try to enhance it in the lives of those for whom we do beneficent deeds.

Kant often makes his position sound like a pan-moralism: a view which demands that all our intentional actions be morally motivated, at least in the broad sense of 'moral' which includes obligations of self-improvement and of general beneficence. Recall that in one form, Kant's Categorical Imperative says, "Act *only* on that maxim which you can will to be a universal law" (emphasis added). But must we always be acting on a maxim (a principle of action)? I think not, and I doubt that Kant is committed to thinking otherwise. More likely, in introducing this form of the imperative, he presupposed that its main application concerns situations that *call* for a moral decision. He may also have been *constructing* the reasoning one would do to explain or justify a moral decision retrospectively, as opposed to the perhaps semi-automatic process by which, in the ongoing world of human affairs, we act as practiced moral agents.

To be sure, Kant may also have taken the moral realm, especially as contrasted with that of self-interest, to be primary in the sphere of value. He may have conceived it as the domain where the most important values are realized or betrayed. He also seems to have held, consonantly with this, that moral reasons are always supreme.[12] This should not be said for Aristotle, though he probably did not think that a person of true practical wisdom would ever be forced to choose between fulfilling moral obligation and doing something that is, overall, rational from the point of view of other values. This point is connected with his controversial view that the virtues are unified, roughly in the sense that to have one implies both having all of the others and having a capacity to avoid irreconcilable conflicts between the demands of one and those of any other. On Mill's utilitarianism, of course, hedonic values are supreme; and if we properly pursue their fulfillment, morality can only applaud.

What is perhaps most distinctive about a Kantian integration of life is the stress on respect for persons as rational beings with a special dignity and, in the light of the requirements for respecting this dignity, on internalizing principles that we can rationally will to be universal. We must treat persons, including ourselves, with a certain kind of concern for their well-being, including their happiness; and we must treat them equally. We may not treat even ourselves as mere means, not even as means to such lofty ends as improving the lives of others—which, on a utilitarian scheme applied to a sufficiently suffering world—might be the end that most deserves our energies.[13] Indeed, "To assure one's own happiness is a duty."[14]

The Kantian demand to treat persons as ends need not be understood to entail that we should approach every decision with a set of rules from which we select one or more to apply to the situation at hand. It is to internalize the Categorical Imperative—together with general principles sanctioned by it—in such a way that, at least for moral decisions, a universalizable principle can be formulated that represents the underlying structure of our practical reasoning or operative motivation.[15] Even this internalization view, which allows that many moral decisions be properly made spontaneously without deliberation or reflection, strikes many (including me) as too intellectualist, at least if applied to non-moral decisions.

There is room for reasonable disagreement, however, about the proportion of life's decisions that are moral in the first place or otherwise come under the requirement of universalizability. In any case, some will find the Kantian framework compelling. Many who do not will find one or another aspect of it appealing; and any thoughtful study of it will yield rewards.

Theological Integration and the Ethics of Love

There is one more way of setting priorities in life that I want to consider here. It is indeed the most common and, for many people, the most compelling way to frame values. It is broadly theological. One might think that this kind of integration would interest only religious people. But even for the non-religious, there is value both in seeing how theological ideals can structure a life and in viewing life from the point of view of an ideal observer, which (among many other things) God can be taken to be. I cannot consider even one theology in detail; and for any major one, there will be significant denominational differences. There will also be room both for individual interpretations of key elements and for a range of ethical views, especially as they bear on non-religious matters.

To fix ideas, let us presuppose a monotheism with the classical triad of elements in Western theism (the theism of Christianity, Judaism, and Islam): God's omniscience (knowledge of all truths), omnipotence (being all-powerful), and omnibenevolence (perfect goodness). And let us assume that a highly developed religion will have scriptures, such as the Bible, as well as religious authorities who interpret them.

We can make the picture more concrete by adding a definite, widely familiar theological supposition. Imagine that I am a "traditional" Christian with a commitment both to my denominational standards and to the basic authority of the Bible, especially the New Testament. Clearly, I am enjoined to love God with all my heart and my neighbor as myself; and I am committed to some version of the Ten Commandments. We could speak here of an *ethics of love*. But although there are acts of love, love itself is not an action, and no one kind of act is required for its expression. There are many ways to develop and express love. Moreover, in saying that we are to love our neighbors as ourselves, Jesus made clear—as Kant and other moral thinkers have—that we *may* (in some sense) love ourselves.[16]

It may be that the force of requiring us to love our neighbors *as ourselves* is to get us to use our pattern of self-concern as a model for treatment of others. We seem to need little if any external incentives, even if we do need a certain kind of upbringing, to pursue our own good. Moreover, where there is the kind of love central in the ethics of love portrayed in the New Testament, there tends to be something else ethically fundamental, particularly in the Kantian tradition. Could we *love* our neighbors in the relevant sense without respecting them as persons? Surely not.

The Ethics of Love and Virtue Ethics

The ethics of love also has a strong connection with virtue ethics. Love (in the sense of lovingness) is not only a good thing, but also, if it is not a virtue in the usual sense of an excellence of character that operates through mastery of standards or skills, it is at least the kind of trait that can account for the development of virtues.[17] Moreover, love leads to a comprehensive range of actions, attitudes, and emotions in a way that might suggest that if a person is sufficiently loving, then given appropriate knowledge and opportunity the person will either develop the other virtues if they are absent or, more likely—since one could hardly be a loving person without some of the other virtues—will act and feel in ways appropriate to those virtues. I am inclined to construe love as indeed a virtue in a person; but perhaps it is a higher order virtue that is not domain-specific in the way the moral virtues tend to be. It applies in every domain of human life, not just that of, say, communication (where veracity is a central virtue) or acknowledgment of what is done for us (where gratitude is a central virtue).

It is possible, however, for love to be both a higher order virtue and the most comprehensive virtue, yet not the "master virtue" in the sense that implies grounding all the other virtues. Consider first whether, in order to be a loving person, one must have certain other virtues. Kindness, for instance, would seem to be required, and perhaps also a degree of generosity. But I do not see that being loving entails being honest, even if it limits the range of cases in which one would deceive, say ruling out cases in which deceit can be seen to be cruel. Love might, in some people, increase the tendency to lie for the apparent good of those they love, for instance to protect the future of their children. It could turn out, however, that love is the most important single virtue, even if it is not the master virtue. This would give it great importance both in ethics and as a central basis for structuring human life.

Like the virtue of lovingness, the love commandments have a correspondingly broad scope. They also provide latitude to pursue quite different kinds of lives. In addition to leaving much room to interpret the Scriptures (the commandments occur in both the Old and New Testaments) to determine what is required of us, these principles leave open many concrete *priorities*. Granted, Christians who want to know what kind of life best fulfills the commandments must read the Bible with the teachings of Jesus foremost in their minds, with close attention to him as a role model, and with a serious effort to understand other parts of the New Testament and indeed the Old as well. To do all this is very difficult; but, within certain limits, it allows for many kinds of lives. Many different careers are possible; many kinds of relationships—within the constraints of love of others—may be cherished; and (as chapter 4 will bring out), varying sociopolitical structures may be favored. The same *kinds* of difficulties and options are likely to characterize other rich religious traditions.

The diversity of lives compatible with Christianity does not imply that there are no required priorities for Christians. A commitment to action to relieve suffering and a respect for human rights will be high priorities for any Christian, as for many others.[18] But a plurality of good lives will be open to Christians; a wide variety of lifestyles, careers, charities, and avocational pursuits will be consonant with Christianity, as with Judaism, Islam, and Eastern religions. Let me suggest, however, something that can help in determining both what is consistent with various kinds of religious commitments and, for religious people, in setting priorities in life.

Theology and Ethics

Recall the assumption that, for at least Christianity, Judaism, and Islam, God is omniscient, omnipotent, and omnibenevolent. And note that this world is plainly one in which there is so much evil that even some who conscientiously try to find God, or evidences of divine sovereignty, fail. If we take the world to be created by God conceived in terms of these three attributes, it is reasonable to think that God would provide ways by which, using reason, such conscientious people can discover at least basic moral and other normative standards necessary for civilized life. These include standards for loving others as oneself. I have argued elsewhere that this discovery is possible in any case, but my point here is that theists (who see God as omniscient, omnipotent, and omnibenevolent) should expect it.[19] Why is this so?

It seems at best unlikely that a perfectly good God would create a world in which some good people conscientiously try to find God or evidences of divine sovereignty and fail, yet there is no way for them to discover basic moral truths and other normative standards essential for civilized life. To create such a world would be to compound the incalculable loss of failing to recognize one's creator with the tragedy of lacking an adequate guide in conducting one's secular life in a way appropriate to creatures of God. If such moral and valuational knowledge is possible independently of theology—and made possible by God—then as a religious person I should realize that non-religious people can acquire it, and I should myself be interested in ascertaining the relevant grounds for such important knowledge. Through this effort I can achieve a *theo-ethical equilibrium*: an integration of my religiously inspired ethical views with the ethical views I find reasonable on the basis of the secular reflection possible for all rational beings.

Achieving this integration may lead me to revise either my theology *or* my secularly developed ethics. Neither domain need automatically have priority in one's thinking, though if basic moral principles are, as Ross held, self-evident, this will tend to give them a certain kind of priority.[20] Equilibrium may be achieved by any number of different combinations of theologically grounded and secularly grounded views. Suppose I take the position, as have St. Thomas Aquinas and many others, that basic moral truths are the necessary kind that, like mathematical truths and the moral truth that (apart from a few exceptions such as self-protection) we should not kill, *cannot* fail to hold.[21] These may be taken to be inherent in the divine mind; they are thus *in* God, not *above* God. They are constants in divine thinking in the same way mathematical truths are, and hence hold in any world God might create.

On the view I am sketching, one may sometimes properly think that ethical inquiry can illuminate theology at least as much as theology can illuminate ethics. In this way, a fruitful interaction between secular reflection and religiously inspired thinking—and indeed religious experience—is achievable. The secular thinking may, up to a point, be Aristotelian, Kantian, utilitarian, or intuitionist. We again find that different approaches can be combined in a variety of ways. This is not because there are no universally valid normative standards. It is because those there are, such as morally and theologically basic principles, can, within limits, be interpreted differently in different situations and with different overall theories of their integration.

4. The Challenge of Cultural Differences and Clashing Worldviews

Does the pluralism I affirm amount to status relativism all over again? Must we countenance just any coherent set of priorities? No: certain basic elements must figure in any good life—or at least any life that is both morally permissible and social rather than solitary.[22] First, in any such life, certain moral standards must be respected, particularly minimal standards of justice, freedom, and happiness (where the notion of happiness is understood broadly and is close to that of well-being). Second, obligations must be met, and here I reiterate the Rossian duties as including most of our central moral obligations: obligations of fidelity and veracity, beneficence and non-injury, gratitude and self-improvement, and reparation and justice. Third, at least a substantial proportion of basic values must be realized to some degree. Among these values I count at least these kinds: hedonic values (constituting a wide spectrum with pleasure at the positive end and pain at the negative end), moral values, intellectual values, aesthetic values, spiritual and religious values, social values, emotional values, and athletic values.

I have spoken of most of these values and indicated that they overlap. There is often pleasure in, for instance, listening to Mozart's *Jupiter;* but there could be aesthetic value in listening to it even if that were not pleasurable (and perhaps even if it were to *some* degree unpleasant). In calling a value basic I mean only that it is not reducible to any other value or to combinations of others, not that its realization cannot be *combined* with that of others.[23]

If we reflect on this list of values, we can see why a good life, though it must realize some of them to a substantial degree, need not realize all of them. One *could* have a good life without realizing values that are properly termed *athletic* and arguably without realizing values properly termed *intellectual.* But this point about the intellectual and the athletic is a misleading truth. For even if there can be a good life without realization of one or the other of these values, a life in which, other things equal, they are both realized is far better. In general, the best life is one that realizes as fully and as coherently as possible the entire gamut of values accessible to us. This broad ideal needs clarification.

First, I speak of values *accessible* to us to frame a realistic ideal. Some people have no capacity to enjoy sports; others lack sight and cannot enjoy painting. Nearly everyone has some significant limitation in regard to experiencing one or another form of goodness. Second, in speaking of the fullest possible realization of values, I have in mind a *roughly* quantitative notion: the more we have in the way of pleasures, intellectual rewards, aesthetic satisfactions, loving relationships, and so forth, the better, other things equal. We have to say 'other things equal' because pleasure can be outweighed by pain it may cause; the rewards of love may be smothered by the bitterness of hate it may arouse in someone hurt by an abandonment; and the satisfactions of contemplating beauty in art may be discolored by the revulsion of ugliness one must endure on the way to the gallery.

We also have to say 'other things equal' for another reason. This brings us to coherence. The goodness of a life, like the beauty of a painting, is organic: the value of the whole can be more or less than the sum of the values of the parts or aspects.[24] In an optimally good life, the parts hang together; they befit one another. We want our loving relationships to be with good people, our aesthetic satisfactions to be taken in activities we do not morally disapprove of, our moral gratifications to come in doing the positive things we take to be significant and not just in preventing evils.[25]

Given how much we differ, and given the diversity of cultures in which people live, one could say that what constitutes a good life is relative to the kinds of people we are talking about and to their opportunities in life. What we have here is not a deep relativity, but a large set of options. Choice among these *is* significantly relative to personal grounds. If one is fond of the idea of relativity, one could speak of *preferential relativism:* the view that where there is a range of equally meritorious permissible options (options permitted by sound moral standards), choice among them may reasonably be determined by personal preference.

Great diversity, however, is compatible with recurring strands in the fabric of the different lives we pursue. Given how much alike we are in potential to realize the basic kinds of value, one could also say that there are certain basic, universally valuable constituents of a life of human flourishing— a good life, in other terms—and that we simply realize them in different ways. This is pluralism. There are universal values, but they are realizable in a multitude of ways. Different cultures favor different combinations and weightings among them; but it is difficult, if possible at all, to find any culture in which the values I have listed do not have a significant place. If there should be a culture in which a significant number did not, it would not constitute a *civilization*.

A civilization, as opposed to a mere group of people living together in a coordinated social structure, is marked by some significant degree of education as well as by institutions and other products of creative invention. The greater the prevalence of an education in the arts and sciences—a liberal education—the richer the civilization tends to be. The point of such an education is in part to widen understanding of the elements that contribute to a life of flourishing and to enhance the capacity to live that life. The rationale for a free democracy is in part to allow people to achieve their own integration of values without undermining the social harmony—or at least stability—needed for people of radically different preferences to do this. Democracy works best where liberal education is widespread and where a kind of basic equality among persons is upheld. But equality is not uniformity. Like happiness, which is a cross-cultural good that is realized in multiple cultural forms, our equal right to liberty is exercised in a multitude of different pursuits.[26]

There is much more to say about how the ethical standards and the theory of value I have presented can work in a free democracy. It is particularly difficult to find a way to make room for conflicting religious worldviews without making it too easy for the expression of one—or its legal imposition if its members become a dominant majority—to abridge the freedom to express another religious worldview. It is also not obvious how the evaluative framework I have developed can help us with the numerous challenges to ethical thinking that the current world presents: not only problems concerning church and state and, more broadly, the religious and secular in individual conduct, but the gap between ethics and technology; the self-indulgence and insularity of so many people; the insufficiency of good role models, especially in the media; and the associated problems of a low level of discourse, of the atrophy of the mind in some of the elderly, and, on the international scene, of global injustice. All of these difficulties and challenges must be faced if the kinds of good lives I have sketched are to be achievable in the future. Some important ethical standards for dealing with them have now been set out. My aim in the final chapter will be to propose some strategies for meeting the major challenges in question.

4

HUMAN DIVERSITY AND DEMOCRATIC INSTITUTIONS

I have so far represented human reason as capable of revealing basic moral principles, experience as the raw material of life from which patterns of value develop, and individuals as the central concern of ethics. But individuals do not flourish as isolated atoms. We do best living in communities, guided by each other and challenged by institutional demands. Like individuals, institutions vary greatly, even when they operate fully within the constraints of morality and sound values. But just as pluralism at the individual level does not imply that there are no universally valid standards of individual conduct, institutional pluralism is compatible with universally valid principles of social ethics and of political obligation.

I am particularly interested in the kinds of institutions that are or, historically, have tended to be central in free democracies: universities, churches, the press and other media, and the main branches of government, especially the legislative and judicial. I can address only a few of these institutions; but it is important to consider some normative standards that apply to them, as well as standards that apply directly just to individuals. Even if individual ethics is more basic than institutional ethics, we cannot structure our lives as individuals or function as morally responsible citizens without taking account of institutional ethics.

1. The Nature of Institutions

Modern life is pervaded by institutions: educational, cultural, religious, legal, financial, and many other kinds. Any of these may influence huge numbers of people, and they are essential elements in dealing with the ethical challenges of contemporary life. Some of them, such as educational or religious institutions, are central in the lives of some people. Many institutions have the potential to endure indefinitely. This gives them a special importance in an age in which many people are not religious. For some, institutions offer the only hope of lasting remembrance. Colleges and universities, scholarships and lecture series, and libraries and museums can endure for centuries—in principle, forever. Through their entire history, they can carry the names of donors and those they honor, and for as long as they exist, they can keep some of their founders' concerns or ideas alive.

What is an institution? Universities are paradigm cases, but an institution can be more abstract than a university. Think of the two-party political system in the United States, which has no property or equipment, or the institution of legal punishment, which can exist for indefinitely long periods on the basis of its recognition rather than its actions. One institution can also be part of a larger one, as a branch of a university is part of the larger multi-campus university system or, perhaps, as a neighborhood church or synagogue or mosque is a local institution belonging to the wider one constituting its denomination. An institution may be as small as a foundation with two employees. Institutions might also include certain political parties and probably certain corporations, such as the BBC or perhaps even IBM, provided they have certain sorts of social roles.

Even apart from the problem of the vagueness of the notion of an institution, definition is difficult.[1] An institution must have some purposive unity, and this commonly involves its relating to people outside it, whether they are a kind of constituency or not. Think of a university or a church. We might conceive an institution as, very roughly, a historically established rule-governed social structure with a unifying purpose of a certain kind and some degree of autonomy.[2] Some unifying purposes are complex. Some purposes also unify those who share them better than others do. In any case, an institutional structure is *purposive* (teleological), at least in the sense that there is a central goal or set of goals. The fulfillment of these goals determines how successful the institution is, and the degree to which they unify its rules determines how well unified it is.[3]

This rough characterization calls for comment. The requirement of historical establishment reflects the realistic assumption that institutions are *founded* or, occasionally, simply grow from the fertile soil of cooperative activity that ultimately yields the requisite structure and rules.[4] The historicity requirement is needed to distinguish institutions taken in the abstract—as rule-governed structures of roles and purposes, which we might call *institution concepts*—from institutions in the concrete, which constitute *instantiations* of those abstract structures. It is the historical realizations in space and time that we have in mind when we ordinarily speak of institutions; and if an institution concept has no such realization, then it is preferable to speak simply of the relevant institution in the abstract.[5] Such abstractions are not historical entities.

A university, for example, is instantiated by—though not identical with—faculty, students, and other role-players, and it normally has physical resources, such as buildings. Compare a statue composed of marble having a certain shape. If, over time, as the statue is moved and damaged, all the marble is replaced bit by bit, we have the same statue composed of different marble. A university, however, is not constituted (or even composed) by its members and their relations. It has reality apart from them. It can cease to be instantiated (or "embodied") after its founding, as where all its members die and its buildings are destroyed, but the relevant documents for reopening remain. A university and its ideas can live forever. Institutions need not remain where they are or even on earth (the future may show that the universe, not the sky, is the limit). Not only can a university exist, like a disassembled watch, with its parts temporarily separated and their functions suspended; unlike a watch, an institution can exist wholly disembodied. (This may sound like theology, but it's really just metaphysics.)[6]

An institution, then, is not identical with its members and its physical embodiment operating together under its constitutive rules. But—and this point is morally crucial—its *actions* are grounded in those of representative members. If an institution is in one sense—the conceptual sense—essentially an abstract structure, institutions as established in the world have concrete elements, and their *actions* are essentially concrete deeds. People are its *base*; it has no agency apart from them. Its actions are their actions *as* performed in accordance with the appropriate rules.

People are also characteristically the proper beneficiaries of institutional activities. In all of this, an institution is like a corporation and unlike a mere collection of people or even a structured group with common purposes, such as a profession: even when all the members of such a group do something, this does not thereby count as a social action in the way that a university official's admitting students counts as its accepting them. Even if all teachers contributed to environmental causes, this would not count as the teaching profession's acting officially; a teacher's professional *association* could perhaps do that, but mere unanimity in environmental support would not count as such.

2. Institutional Ethics in Pluralistic Democracies

Precisely because institutions act through individuals who appropriately represent them, they are capable of good and bad conduct and, implicitly, of both virtue and vice. In addition, in a free democracy many kinds of institutions—and perhaps all the "public" ones—are citizens, crucial citizens, though they lack a political vote in the ordinary sense.[7] We can thus expect that there should be such a thing as institutional ethics and indeed institutional citizenship. What this requires will vary with type of institution.

In part because institutions act through the persons who play certain roles in them, institutional ethics mirrors individual ethics. For instance, negatively, institutions have obligations of non-injury, including the avoidance of injustice and of unwarranted restriction of liberty. Positively, they have obligations of fidelity to promises, of honesty, and (in my view) of beneficence. These in turn imply an obligation of those who control an institution to live up to the appropriate institutional purposes: not to do so would be faithless or dishonest or both.

It is in the *application* of obligations that we find the chief difference with the individual case: moral obligations apply only indirectly to institutions, *via* the duties of relevant role players. This point helps us to see the difference between institutional vice and institutional virtue. In an ethically sound institution, there is an interactive spirit of moral commitment; role players have a sense of duty regarding their own institutional domain and some sense of how roles related to their own should be played; and their attitudes and behavior bear an appropriate relation to the overall purposes of the institution. Ideally, there is teamwork or at least mutual support. In an ethically unsound institution, by contrast, there is self-seeking, rationalization when immorality occurs, passing the buck to some other role player, and much else that is familiar from the history of corrupt institutions.

An important ethical implication of these points is that we must educate people for their roles in institutions and not just to govern their conduct as individuals. Institutional conduct is crucial for solving the kinds of major problems besetting the United States and many other countries today. Moreover, even if other "collectives," such as civic organizations, sports teams, and active communities are not always institutions, they share a similar kind of moral responsibility. Sections 3 and 4 will develop the general idea of institutional ethics and citizenship and, against that background, we can consider the major problems sketched in chapter 1 that pose challenges to ethics.

3. Institutional Citizenship and Political Responsibility

Private as well as public institutions have moral obligations, particularly negative obligations such as not to kill, injure, lie, or break promises. But if an institution is public and paid for by taxes, as in the case of public radio and TV and many universities, positive obligations, especially to do certain good deeds, are prominent, and they may be owed to a wide public. Indeed, in a complex modern economy, almost any institution may have public support at least in the form of tax relief.

Where institutions have public support, it will often be by virtue of their commitment to playing a certain socially approved role. Consider public radio. It is likely to have both a mission statement and enabling legislation that partly determine its obligations to the public. Something similar applies to public educational institutions. Churches, however, gain tax relief (hence public support) in a different way—in part because they are charitable and in part because taxing them would potentially restrict their activities in a way that a free society is reluctant to do. In their case, then, obligations to the public are chiefly *internally defined*. Some of the implications of this special position will be considered shortly.

Even if institutions had only negative obligations, there would still be a sense in which they are citizens. They are governed by and benefit from the protections of an ordered society—indeed, one might posit a kind of tacit social contract here as a way of determining obligations on both sides. Perhaps more important, institutions are mainly constituted by citizens who have all the normal moral obligations to others implied by ordinary citizenship. But where institutions are either publicly funded or play a major public role, citizenship becomes an even more important aspect of their function.

There is one dimension of this citizenship I particularly want to explore. Citizenship in a free democracy implies playing a potential role in public discourse, particularly discourse important for public policy and political decision, and a readiness to play such a role. This role can be seen to be ethically appropriate on any of the major ethical views we have considered. Recall the intuitive obligations stressed by ethical intuitionism. These include the obligation to contribute to human happiness, though the pluralism of any common-sense intuitionism makes this only one among other obligations. Utilitarianism makes it central. The Kantian demand that we treat persons as ends and avoid treating them merely as means also applies to institutions. Sound institutional ethics is essential for any society and particularly for free democracies. With the news media, the need is constant. Let us explore it.

4. News Media

An essential element in the role of the news media in free democracies is reporting on government. A central problem in journalistic ethics is how the press should balance merely providing information about government and, on the other hand, giving the government in its own country blanket approval, or uncritically supporting a particular political party, whether or not it is in power. In Aristotelian terms, in informing the public about politics and government, news media must find a mean between the excesses of the ferocious bloodhound and the deficiencies of the somnolent watchdog. A good theory in social-political philosophy should provide at least the main normative standards appropriate to solving this problem of balance.

In part, the solution is for the press to preserve a *division of function*. The reporting function is one thing and the editorial is another, though the two are related and must be coordinated. The reliability of a newspaper's reporting should not depend on its politics. The same holds for radio and TV stations. In editorials, however, the press may appropriately have a political voice. On some accounts, it should, or even must, have a political voice, perhaps on the ground that a democracy needs media with opposing political views. On another view, the press should see that opposing views are appropriately represented but refuse to be closely identified with any of them. In any case, to *have* a political voice is not to *be* one. The press must not be just a political instrument.

The standard is different for the news office of an educational institution, and branches of government may also have press offices. But the major function of the press in a free society should not be subordinate to any government agency and preferably not even to a major institution whose main purpose is non-journalistic, as is, for instance, the promotion of a labor union or of one or another industry. Journalists should never be summed up by their politics. They must preserve their autonomy in and beyond the political realm.

This is one reason why great care must be taken in structuring a system of government support for news media. Private support—particularly from advertising revenue—can also be a threat to journalistic independence. But, other things equal, it seems better that support be private than that it be governmental, and that the private sources be more rather than less diverse. If a radio station is dependent on a single donor, how independent can we expect it to be? If, however, there are competing stations each supported by a single donor or category of donors, this may offset the imbalance there would otherwise be. That source of balance is limited, however, by the distribution of wealth in a society. This distribution may be such as to make government support—of a non-partisan kind—desirable or even necessary.

The news media, and indeed the wider media, can play a major role in dealing with the moral problems of our age. Some of these problems concern their own functioning; the media, like individuals, may and should be self-critical. I will return to such problems in discussing contemporary ethical challenges.

5. A Framework for Approaching Moral Problems in Free Democracies

In the context of the overall ethical perspective now set out, I want to address the ten pressing contemporary ethical problems sketched in chapter 1. I do not claim that no others are equally serious. But these are quite enough to discuss here; and for those who want to probe further, each of them suggests a number of other problems. All of these problems are connected with institutions: where they are not largely problems of institutional behavior, they are treatable within the scope of activity of many institutions, particularly those in the media.

My own ethical view has a number of implications for these problems. In the most general terms, it implies an obligation to enhance the quality and quantity of human happiness in a framework of scrupulous liberty and justice. In less general terms, it affirms, as guiding us in fulfilling this obligation, the intuitive Rossian obligations: above all, non-injury and justice, fidelity and reparation, beneficence and self-improvement, and gratitude. I cannot now systematically derive the implications of this ethical position, but I will make a number of points in the hope of generating constructive thinking about the challenges to be addressed.

Religion and the State

This problem concerns the proper balance between governmental and religious institutions. Since preservation of religious liberty is a main concern of free democracies, the state should not interfere with churches—by which I mean religious institutions in general. I propose three principles: first, a *liberty principle*—implicit in the pluralist universalism formulated in chapter 1—which says that (within tolerant limits) the state should permit the free exercise of religion; second, an *equality principle*, which says that the state should give no preference to one religion over another; and third, a *neutrality principle*, which says that the state should be neutral with respect to religion. Here are a few points of rationale.

The liberty principle is needed to protect citizens against governmental *coercion* in religious matters, though it does allow some state restrictions, such as prohibitions of human sacrifice. A free democracy is not morally bound to allow major harms to persons in the name of religion. The equality principle is needed to protect citizens against governmental *discrimination*, as where a majority religion is allowed to dominate certain kinds of public office—something possible even given religious liberty. The neutrality principle is needed to prevent governmental *favoritism* of the religious over the non-religious.

Favoritism can occur even if no one religion is preferred over any other. Indeed, even if there is nothing that would be uncontroversially called *discrimination* against the non-religious, a measure of favoritism of the religious is possible. Suppose, for instance, that the religious have preference in certain government appointments provided other things are equal. Thus, if a religious person is as well qualified for such an appointment as a non-religious person, the former would be appointed. Then competition may be free and— some would argue—in a certain sense not unfair, since a non-religious person *better* qualified than a religious competitor would never fail to be preferred over the latter. Still, the former would not have an *equal chance* of appointment, and this seems unfair given our assumption that the qualifications for the appointment are not religious. The point holds, though with less force, even if the favoritism operating when others things equal ceases once a limited proportion of the appointments are filled by religious people (say the proportion they represent in the population).[8] Similar issues arise for certain affirmative action policies, where some degree of preference is given to minority or female candidates, but I do not have space to pursue that issue separately.

The liberty and equality principles are reflected in the First Amendment of the U.S. Constitution, which prohibits Congress from establishing a religion or prohibiting free exercise of religion. The liberty principle is essentially stated therein; the equality principle is arguably the main underlying standard supporting the establishment clause.[9] Let us assume that the Founders who wrote the Constitution were wise to prohibit an established church. This prohibition does not entail *religious neutrality* in the sense of governmental neutrality toward the religious and the *non*-religious, but it does indirectly support such neutrality. Should a free democracy observe the neutrality principle as well as the liberty and equality principles? This issue is very much alive in the United States today and is also important for other democracies.

It is partly in the name of neutrality that many in the United States (religious as well as non-religious) resist requiring or even allowing the idea of intelligent design to be introduced in science education as an alternative to the theory of evolution in explaining the biological development of the human species. Supposing (controversially) that this idea is theistic, giving it required space in the curriculum still need not breech the equality principle; but, as involving government in teaching or promoting religion, it would breach the neutrality principle.[10] In fact, however, many religious people believe that the requirement would in effect favor fundamentalist denominations and hence violate the equality principle. This view cannot be assessed here, but it has enough plausibility to indicate that, in practice, observing the equality principle is at best difficult without observing the neutrality principle.

For a contrasting case of great contemporary interest, consider the government's providing vouchers to enable students who object to public schooling to attend private schools that charge tuition. Arguably, this practice is consistent with neutrality in that it applies equally to religious and non-religious students: the state simply provides funds for *any* student to attend a private school, whether religious or secular, that meets normal educational standards.

There is a related church-state matter not addressed by the Constitution. If, as one might expect proponents of the First Amendment to hold, the state should not interfere with the church, it is also true that the church should not interfere with the state. This is not only because one religious group might, at least if it represents a majority of the citizens, dominate other religious groups. It is also because the institutional integrity of churches is best preserved if their spiritual and moral missions are not diluted by political preoccupations. Here, then, I suggest a *principle of ecclesiastical political neutrality*: In a free democracy, churches committed to being institutional citizens in such a society have some obligation (a prima facie obligation) to abstain from supporting candidates for public office or pressing for laws or public policies that restrict human conduct (this of course includes most laws). This principle does not hamper moral or spiritual leadership. Granted, there is no sharp distinction between the political and the moral, but many clergy in the United States, at least, voluntarily follow this principle.

Religious Sensibilities and Individual Citizenship

Related to the church-state problem is one that arises for individual citizens, as opposed to institutions such as churches and branches of government. In light of what I have said about individual and institutional ethics, and about the plural grounds of values and of moral standards, it is appropriate to begin with four further points about the relation between ethics and religion.

First, moral principles like the kind formulated in chapter 1 can certainly receive support from religious scriptures and institutions, though I do not think that they *must* receive such support in order to deserve allegiance. Certain moral principles can be seen to be reasonable in the light of non-religious arguments, even if they could gain wider and differently grounded support from certain religious considerations.[11] This is not to say that we may always expect people to be adequately *motivated* to be moral without the help of religious commitments; I believe many can be, but how many kinds of people and under what conditions are empirical questions on which we need more data. Certainly religious commitments have often been a source of strong motivation to be moral, but, just as clearly, there are rigorously moral people who are not religious.

Second, the support between ethics and religion can in fact be mutual: secular moral argument can also confirm religiously commanded moral principles and can enhance the resolve to abide by them. Indeed, on the assumption that God is omniscient and omnibenevolent—all-knowing and all-good— *any* cogent argument, including an utterly non-religious one,

for a moral principle *is* in effect an argument for God's know-
ing, and hence (as wholly good) mandating (though not compelling) conformity to, that principle. Why would God not
(in some sense) mandate or require our conformity to a true
moral principle?[12]

A third point is that the overall, triple-barreled moral
principle I have suggested and the everyday principles of obligation I have affirmed as falling under it are quite consistent with the main ethical teachings of at least the Hebraic-
Christian tradition. This is in part because those teachings
articulate some of the universally valid moral standards that
(I would argue) any fully rational person can arrive at with
sufficient information and adequate reflection.

A fourth point emerges when we consider cases in which a
morally mature religious tradition goes beyond secular ethical
principles in requiring *more* from us. When this happens, the
standard is often consistent with those principles. Take the
Christian emphasis on extensive giving to the poor. Living
up to this requires meeting a high standard of conduct that,
though consistent with universally respected secular moral
standards, is not entailed by them. Suppose, however, that a religious command prohibits conduct that secular morality allows, such as using contraceptives. A free, democratic society
will have principles of separation of church and state that, on
the one hand, respect such a prohibition for those who believe
in it but, on the other hand, disallow imposing the prohibition
by law.

What about the sometimes tragic case of an individual
caught between a religion that prohibits a deed, such as assisted suicide, and a reasonable morality that permits it?
Given the unlimited possibilities for dealing with such opposing demands, tragic cases like these can usually be avoided.
But if they cannot be, ethical reflection does not automatically yield a resolution. This is a question best answered by
practical wisdom exercised from the general point of view of
rationality. And reason does not always give a clear answer, or

the same answer, in these hard cases. For some people, reflection may bring a secular moral permission into conformity with a religious prohibition by reinterpretation of the religious standard; for others, or indeed for the same people on other occasions, the resolution may come through revising the secular permission.

With all this in mind, let me suggest a moderate principle applicable to individual conduct and meant to preserve both religious sensibility and civic harmony. This *principle of secular rationale* says that citizens in a free democracy have a prima facie obligation not to advocate or support any law or public policy that restricts human conduct unless they have, and are willing to offer, adequate secular reason for this advocacy or support, e.g. for a vote favoring legal restriction of conduct.[13] Two comments are needed immediately. First, a prima facie obligation (as explained in chapter 1) is not absolute, but defeasible; hence the obligation expressed here can in special cases, such as the need to prevent the rise of a brutal dictator, be overridden. Second, a secular reason is roughly a reason whose evidential force, that is, ability to justify, does not depend on—but also does not deny—the existence of God and, more broadly, does not depend on theological considerations (or on the pronouncements of a person or institution *as* a religious authority).[14]

If, given the usual assumption of God's omniscience and omnibenevolence, there is as much reason to expect alignment between religiously based and secularly based moral principles as I have suggested, then following the principle of secular rationale should not pose insurmountable problems for most religious people. In particular, it does not restrict freedom of *expression*. Its concern is restricting coercion. It leaves open just when it is or is not desirable to bring religious considerations into one's conversation or public discourse.

The positive suggestion is partly this: as citizens in a free democracy, we may be as inspired as we like by our religious insights and tradition, but when it comes to deciding on how *we* as a pluralistic, multicultural society should live—particularly when it comes to prohibiting what others think they have a right to do—we should have some adequate reason that any rational, adequately informed citizen can appreciate independently of having the religion or culture or idiosyncratic nature of those who offer it. This principle is supportable, I would add, by the virtually universally accepted religious commandment: "Do unto others as you would have them do unto you." Nothing galls us like the sense that, for other people's religious reasons, we must do what they want.

This is not in the least to suggest that there are no religious reasons for ethical conduct that are good by any reasonable standard. The Bible and other religious scriptures contain both sound moral principles and many narratives that embody sound moral standards. Indeed, the principle of secular rationale is quite consistent with a plausible counterpart principle applicable to religious citizens whose religions have (as do such major religious as Christianity, Judaism, and Islam) ethical standards that apply to large segments of sociopolitical conduct. This *principle of religious rationale* says: In a free democracy, religious citizens have a prima facie obligation not to advocate or support any law or public policy that restricts human conduct, unless they have, and are willing to offer, adequate *religiously acceptable* reason for this advocacy or support.[15] The acceptability in question is understood to be internal to the religion of the citizens in question.

The principle of religious rationale presupposes that (for rational persons) ethics has a certain internal application within a religion. The principle asks us to give weight to considerations we are committed to living by, even if they are internal to a practice or institution that is not universal. Such considerations may still be harmonious with ethical standards that are universally valid. Religious considerations may indeed add greatly to a person's grounds or motivation (or both) to realize those standards.

Consider assisted suicide again. If I oppose it on religious grounds, this might be because I think that only God gives life and only God should take it. But if I think about voting to illegalize it on this basis, it should occur to me that people who disapprove, from *their* religious point of view, of things I believe I have a right to do might abridge my legal rights if they were in a majority and they acted on my principle. Given how religious majorities can change, this is a realistic worry in many parts of the world, and especially where religious fundamentalists support restrictions that others—religious as well as secular—reject.

There is another reason why I might hesitate to illegalize assisted suicide. Suppose I am Christian and reflect on the principle of religious rationale. It may then occur to me to question whether, for instance, "Thou shalt not kill" is meant to include suicide. I may also be aware that many whose scripture is the Bible do not see it as condemning *all* suicides and take reason as a gift from God for the direction of human life—including the manner of our dying if remaining alive would otherwise lead to indignity, extreme suffering, and heavy use of scarce resources. It may also seem obvious (as perhaps it is) that a sound ethics reflects what we might call a *proxy rights principle*: if you have a right to do something but *cannot* do it without help, then you have a secondary right to ask a willing person (such as a physician) to provide the means or bring about the end.[16]

The Gap between Ethics and Technology

The religious sensibilities problem leads naturally to another I have mentioned: the gap between ethics and technology. Much of the deepest opposition to various technological advances comes from religiously grounded moral standards, for example those implying that cloning, especially of human beings, encroaches on the divine plan. But even apart from religious scruples, we can be concerned about the invasions of privacy that are possible given how much information is on computers and subject to ready transfer, copying, and, in some cases, piracy by hackers. These invasions are increasingly likely given the threat of terrorism. Governments as well as individuals may violate privacy rights. From the basic principles favoring maximal liberty and prohibiting injury and injustice, it is clear that there are strong moral incentives to restrict invasions of privacy from any direction.

Whatever the source of our worries about technological advances, it is essential that we get ethics ahead of technology. This is a special challenge for institutional ethics. Institutions (including certain corporations) are probably the chief sources of technical advances. Both in educational institutions and in private life we must teach ethics widely and emphatically. We must put ethical problems on the regular agenda of research and development. And we must not undermine the guiding effects of ethics by calling it subjective or saying that "everything is relative," as if there were no rational choice to be made concerning how we should constrain the use of new technologies.[17] The current world climate is perhaps unfavorable for curtailing some of our most dangerous technologies, including those in the military and nuclear power spheres. It does seem favorable for enhancing the use of technology in, say, education and health care. Cloning, however, is a practice that in some parts of the world is not well regulated; and although it is widely agreed that human beings should not be cloned, it is not clear exactly what restrictions should be placed on other kinds of cloning.

A related challenge is this. Research is coming closer to enabling easy preselection of the sex of children (determining, before conception and without artificial insemination or expensive medical procedures, what will be the sex of the child-to-be). This is an excellent example of a technology that on the face of it seems unobjectionable but, on reflection, can be seen to be likely to have profound effects in some places.[18] In some countries it may result in a disproportion-ate number of male births, a phenomenon whose impact, in-cluding its effect on the status of women, is difficult to fore-see. The technology might, however, also reduce the birth rate in many cases, since people could have children of the desired sex(es) without having *more* children than they want. This is not to suggest any specific ethical standard for using preselection techniques; but the equal treatment of males and females that ethics requires may in some cases be seri-ously threatened by preselection technology. To be sure, some uses of the technique appear to be protected under the maximization of liberty clause in the pluralist universalism proposed in chapter 1; but specifying these and indicating certain limitations is too large a task to undertake here. My main point is instead that there should be discussion with clear and publicized conclusions—and disagreements—before such a technology is made widely available.

Universities that do research with human subjects quite properly use review boards, and these often coordinate their inquiries with the deliberations of ethics committees. We may surely ask industry to step up its concern with ethical matters. This is not to suggest that there is presently no concern in in-dustry; but we have seen too often (as, on many views, with cloning) how the momentum of technology and the incentive of profit lead to morally questionable developments. To call for ethical concerns to be brought to bear in the development and not just the use of technology is not even necessarily to ask for economic sacrifices. The effect on industrial profits is not obvious. It might be positive more often than negative.

Mental Atrophy and the Graying of Advanced Societies

The next problem I want to address is one of the most acute of our time, and it illustrates how technology can bring to the fore

a moral issue that previously arose much less frequently. I refer
to the tragedy of the body's outliving the mind. Too often, the
mind dies before the brain. Above all, we need more and better
education and better utilization of the retired and elderly. Humanistic education, for instance in philosophy and literature,
is especially useful; for it is education not just for careers but
for free time and retirement—even for dry or stressful periods
between jobs. People must be taught to use their minds on a
wide and unpredictable variety of problems, and they must be
able to *enjoy* exercising their intellectual equipment. This may
be the best defense there is against mental atrophy. It is ironic
that nourishing and exercising the body is so fashionable while
the mind, which also needs nourishment and exercise, is often
taken for granted, even when it is weak and underfed.

The need to resist mental atrophy is a central concern
from the point of view of virtue ethics. Mental capacity is
essential for development and even maintenance of the various excellences of character. The Rossian obligation of self-
improvement also directs us to fight against atrophy. These
imperatives are not utopian. Much more can be done to provide opportunities for the elderly and retired to help both
one another and the young. Older people can serve as tutors
in academic pursuits, trainers in occupational tasks, helpers
in child care, and advisors of younger adults. Indifference
or prejudice toward the elderly is one kind of immorality;
slothfulness on the part of the healthy retired is, arguably, the
other side of the coin. The massive involvement I suggest
could help to overcome both, and, combined with incentives
toward earlier retirement, or at least early partial retirement,
might reduce unemployment. Grants and tax incentives would
help with this problem, but one would hope that even apart
from them, a stronger social ethics would suffice.

Colleges and universities, moreover, can often reach out
more effectively to older people, both for the enrichment of
their cultural lives and for their orientation in the various

fields in which they can become supportive volunteers or part-time salaried workers. In addition to educating people for *career change*, as opposed to preparing them for a specialty or some small range of jobs, higher education should help people both to adjust to changes in patterns of living and to prepare for continued vitality in retirement and, for many, in the infirmity of old age.

More than ever before, living well is not fully achievable apart from dying well. Our moral responsibilities extend to the latter as well as the former. In the quest to age gracefully, the humanities are uniquely valuable. Let me illustrate. Dylan Thomas gave us one striking injunction. His "Do Not Go Gentle Into That Good Night" begins:

> Do not go gentle into that good night,
> Old age should burn and rave at close of day,
> Rage, rage against the dying of the light.

And it ends:

> Grave men, near death, who see with blinding sight
> Blind eyes could blaze like meteors and be gay,
> Rage, rage against the dying of the light.

> And you, my father, there on the sad height,
> Curse, bless, me now with your fierce tears, I pray.
> Do not go gentle into that good night,
> Rage, rage against the dying of the light.[19]

Compare this picture with T. S. Eliot's in "The Love Song of J. Alfred Prufrock," in which Prufrock says

> I should have been a pair of ragged claws
> Scuttling across the floors of silent seas

and closes with

> I have heard the mermaids singing, each to each.
> I do not think that they will sing to me . . .

> We have lingered in the chambers of the sea
> By sea-girls wreathed with seaweed red and brown
> Till human voices wake us, and we drown.[20]

There is no rage here, and no zest for continued life. The only animated existence seems to be in fantasy, and even then on the part of truncated human beings. Amid human voices, Prufrock neither sings nor rages; he drowns. It does not have to be like that.

Self-Indulgence

Fifth on my list of contemporary problems that pose special challenges to ethics is *self-indulgence*. There is egocentrism—me-centeredness—in individuals. In communities and nation states, there is excessive concern with one's own circle—or country, or religious group, or tribe—with far too little commitment to helping outsiders. Self-indulgence is not just a tendency that impedes fulfilling responsibilities to others. Pulling against the obligation of self-improvement, it also tends to hurt those it afflicts. It is typically combined with little or no resolve to achieve excellence.

The point is not only that virtues of character cannot be well developed given self-indulgence; many pleasures are also out of reach, those of (for instance) most great literature, much contemporary art, and many kinds of conversation. Other pleasures, including those of self-understanding and many forms of social life, also are inaccessible without some disciplined efforts. Self-indulgence tends to undermine the success of any of the kinds of lives described in chapter 3, even for those who manage to fulfill the minimal ethical obligations directed toward avoiding harm to others. One might object that self-indulgence may be at worst imprudent, but I believe that Kant, Ross, and others who have taken self-improvement to be a moral obligation were correct. From a Kantian point of view, improving ourselves (for the right reasons) is a special case of treating persons as ends. Even from a utilitarian point of view, it tends to enhance happiness.

In America in particular, which makes such heavy use of cars, electricity, and disposable, non-biodegradable materials, insufficient concern with the environment, animals, and future generations is part of this self-indulgence problem. The use of drugs to the point of impairing competence is another part. For self-centered people such as I am imagining, Kant's idea that we should treat persons as ends is alien; others are important not as ends in themselves, but mainly as means.

Self-indulgence must be combated by fighting the selfishness that seems an almost irresistible force in human nature; but we can also help by avoiding the confusion of pluralism with subjectivity. The difference between these has been one of the main points in this book. Diversity, even when it reflects thoughtful disagreement, does not imply that nothing is really good, or that what *is* good is just a matter of taste.

A related ethical point bears on the self-centeredness problem. Recent years have seen a huge emphasis on human rights. This is appropriate given how widely human rights are regularly violated. The vocabulary of rights has a major place in describing abuses and and in framing policies to root them out. But there is another side to this dimension of morality, particularly for the prosperous. If we who live in wealthy advanced societies think too much about our rights, as we may tend to when we face opposition or misfortune, and if we think too little about our responsibilities, we can find ourselves persistently waiting for things to be done for us—often by the government—and frustrated when things are not done for us.

Rights may not only lead to some people's expecting too much to be done for them by others; they may also rationalize inaction by those who need no charity. I suppose I have a right not to vote if I do not want to, yet surely voting is one of my ethical responsibilities. My right not to do it may protect me from being *forced* to; but it gives me no *reason* not to and does not free me from criticism for not doing to. A protection from coercion is not a protection from criticism. A main purpose of a good education is to prepare one for this citizenship role and to nurture a taste for exercising it. Rights are only one side of morality and can sometimes be the self-protective rationalization of the selfish rather than the moral refuge of the downtrodden.[21]

Insularity

Self-indulgence can lead to the sixth problem I have stressed, though this one can afflict even people with much discipline in pursuing what they care about. I refer to insularity, often accompanied by indifference to those perceived as, in one way or another, foreign. In the individual it is ignorance of other times, other places, other ways, and other cultures, and this insularity is often reflected in institutions and the social fabric. At its worst, it breeds not merely a neglect of what is different but a self-satisfied ethnocentrism. People who are insular generally cannot fulfill obligations of beneficence reaching beyond a small circle and are unlikely to fulfill various other obligations, such as those of justice and self-improvement.

The insularity problem can be solved only by changes in both belief and attitude. People must learn more about other times, places, and ways of living. For this, the historical study of the past, the comparative study of the current world, and the philosophical and literary study of alternative possibilities are crucial. These endeavors, being pursuits of knowledge, are mainly cognitive. But they can be reinforced by actual experiences of alternatives to what is familiar, for instance through internships in business or the professions and through work or study in other cultures.

If we should cultivate diversity, should we not also be multicultural? In the best sense of the term, yes: we should seek to understand and not merely tolerate other cultures and subcultures; we should not be self-satisfied about our own ways of doing things; and we should try to relate to people quite different from us. It would be wrong, however, to assume that because we differ from others, we have nothing major in common: we can differ greatly from others and still share basic moral commitments, for instance to justice, freedom, and the promotion of spiritual and material flourishing. To think that cultural differences undermine a common morality is one of the serious mistakes abetted by status relativism. There are not only moral universals. There are also non-moral universals across cultures: birth and death, joy and suffering, love and hate, the need for self-respect, opportunity, and social interactions. These universals have different shapes in different cultures. But between elemental aspects of life like these and our biological similarities, we have enough in common to make communication possible.

The Role Model Problem

So far, I have been talking mainly about the standards, principles, and values important in ethical conduct. But without people who present these and bring them vividly to life, their effectiveness is quite limited. This brings us to the next problem I want to address and, by implication, to an element in the solution of all our major ethical problems. This role model problem is the kind that an Aristotelian ethics would put at center stage. A religiously inspired ethical viewpoint, such as one deriving from the Bible, is likely to do so too. The problem is largely what I have called an insufficiency of good role models: there are either too few exhibiting excellence, or too few with enough influence relative to the ubiquitous bad role models, the exemplars of violence and exploitation, power and ostentation, bigotry and xenophobia.

The importance of the problem is increasing because of the progressively greater access to the Internet and the widening access to popular media. Marketing has become a powerful cultural force, supplying role models as well as the products they allegedly use. It is noteworthy that the power of the media is rising faster than the educational level of people in underdeveloped, often highly populous countries who stand to be heavily influenced by television, radio, and the Internet. The insufficiency of good role models is a problem of great magnitude, but at least *everyone*—including institutions, businesses, and even entire industries—can make some contribution: we can start with ourselves by our own conduct and through efforts to get others to do likewise.

The most influential role models for a great many people, at least early in life, are parents, teachers, and clergy. But others very quickly acquire great influence on us. These include friends, political figures, and of course figures in the media: not just heroes and heroines, but some that we observe every day, people *designed* to make us identify with them—the minutely scripted, often intensely attractive, characters of advertising. The media, including the Internet, are immensely influential in the developed world and are becoming more influential elsewhere.

We should work toward better quality across the board, particularly with a view to enhancing the influence of excellent role models and reducing the number and influence of bad ones. I am not proposing censorship, and I would reject any attempt to reduce the freedom to present diverse models in creative ways. But the media can do better on this score: in movies, drama, advertising, and others areas.[22] Those of us who care about the problem must make ourselves heard more often. It may be that, in America at least, too large a proportion of highly influential role models are entertainers. This is not an unalterable sociological pattern, natural though it is. Here journalists can do more to help. The entertainment media depend on them for credibility; the public stands to be better informed by their reporting.

This is a good place to emphasize a point that may be surprising given my earlier emphasis on secular reasons in the ethics of citizenship. The point is that the area of role models is one in which it is easy to separate church and state too much: neither teaching ethics nor even emphasizing, without indoctrination, the non-religious excellences of great religious figures, violates any reasonable separation of church and state. In the United States and perhaps other developed nations, *moral education* in pre-college public schooling is insufficient. So is the teaching of religion as a major subject of learning: teaching toward understanding as distinct from espousal. Relativism may be more at fault here than overextension of separation of church and state, but the latter can lead some people to think that religion cannot be taught with appropriate intellectual distance. This is an error that, somewhat ironically given the conscientiousness of some who make it, intensifies the effects of relativism. I have indicated some ways to resist both errors.

The Power of the Media and the Function of the Press

My concern here is the media overall, not just the insufficiency of good role models therein—the role model problem extends far beyond the media. We have allowed the media to offer shoddy programs, often violent, offensive to women and minorities, and simplistic in their worldview; and we also tolerate much too thin a coverage of major issues. In an election year in the United States, for example, newspeople have often spent more time reporting on polls and on who is likely to win than on what candidates will do, or should do, if they *do* win. Surely the media gave a disproportionate share of attention in 1995—and even afterward—to the O. J. Simpson murder trial and (later) to Elian Gonzales, the boy who arrived illegally in Florida on a boat from Cuba. Too many other newsworthy events were crowded out or given short shrift.

The style of reporting can be no less important than the amount of coverage given to a story. In April 1996, much media attention was given to the so-called Unabomber, who apparently killed three people and maimed a score. This deserved coverage, but not the proportion received (supplanting many national and international events of general concern, and amounting to lengthy segments on network news and on public radio and TV).

More important, no special efforts were in evidence to prevent what we might call the *celebrity effect* of dramatizing the events. To avoid contributing to this effect, I use 'so-called' rather than allow the apparently self-styled name 'Unabomber' to float free and vie for the glamour its dastardly inventor no doubt wanted. An interesting question of journalistic ethics is how close the media may come in these and other criminal cases to stating the facts in a way that is humiliating to the perpetrator or otherwise calculated to be a disincentive to those who—perhaps influenced by our entertainment media as well—hanker for the sordid limelight such atrocities bring.

More recently, the legal case against popular singer Michael Jackson has received even more attention, as much as about half of the news content of major television network news programs on certain days. An allegation of molesting a child is very serious, but the certainty of child starvation and AIDS infection in Africa and other parts of the world is even more so. This case and similar ones raise the question of what positive standards are central for the news media. Let me cite four standards that are also relevant to some degree to other media.

In free democracies the appropriate ethical standards for journalistic media should be framed in the light of at least four major functions that (as I have elsewhere argued)[23] the press must serve: a political function, providing both information and ideas to the citizenry; a perspectival function, offering a range of conceptions of the shape and texture of the society or certain parts of it (a religious versus a secular one, a conservative versus a liberal one, and so on); a historical function, keeping before us certain traditions and comparisons with the past; and a modeling function, providing and comparing a variety of models of personalities, individual conduct, and institutional structures. Each of these functions is governed by ethical standards that, in ways suggested in this chapter, can be viewed as applications of the common-sense ethical pluralism described in chapter 1.

In connection with the modeling and perspectival functions, it is particularly instructive to reflect on one major domain of human life, especially prominent in America, which both the news and entertainment media cover in great detail. I refer to *sports*. Its bearing on the ethical tone of society has yet to be adequately studied. Sports can teach respect for others, sharing, self-discipline, and a sense of the value of the quest as distinct from that of the prize. It *must* teach a degree of coordination, a capacity for decision under uncertainty, and at least some capacity to tolerate risk, pain, and defeat. I believe that we must make every effort to suffuse sports with ethics and to make early athletic education an ethical training ground.

Role models in sports, particularly but not exclusively professionals, can make a vast difference (as some have).[24] We should call on them to do their best, particularly when on camera, and should criticize them when they fail. (When, in 2000, Myles Brand, then president of Indiana University, fired Bobby Knight, the basketball coach, the reaction from most fans was at best one-sided, and Brand even received threats.) There is also ample opportunity at the grass roots. Parents tend to be the first trainers in sports; elementary school teachers and coaches are next. Moral education can begin here without the least heavy-handedness, and in these contexts it does not require extensive training. What it does require beyond ordinary moral sensitivity can, and I think should, be provided in a good undergraduate education.

As to the myriad bad role models on the screen, on radio, and on the Internet, we also should do all we can to eliminate them—or at least reduce their negative influence. This is not to say that violence and sexual exploits cannot be shown, but they should not be glamorized. Parents should monitor their children's use of the media, particularly the Internet. Many adults should be more selective than they are, for themselves as well as their children. Too many people, at least in the Western world and certainly in America, have come to substitute a passive evening of commercial television for an active evening of, say, conversation or serious reading. But the latter can be as enjoyable as the former, and more richly so.

The large proportion of time many people spend watching television or using the Internet for entertainment is well known to have reduced conversational interaction and even community activities or social life between friends in other households. This tends to reduce what social scientists call "social capital," which represents a kind of value in a community that is a measure of (among other things) the trust, the number and strength of communicative channels, and the potential for the cooperative efforts crucial for democracy. Citizens who agree on the points made here about the media should express themselves, both by criticizing the media for certain kinds of portraits of violence and by publicly boycotting certain products or programs.

Global Justice

What I have said so far applies internationally, but it is mainly directed at encouraging reforms in one country at a time. There is, however, a pressing international problem of global justice. The obligations of justice, like other ethical obligations, are not restricted to any one country or to relations between individuals in only a single nation. A major challenge here is how the developed nations can do more to relieve suffering and overcome ignorance elsewhere. This is an obligation that is especially weighty for utilitarians, but it is serious on any of the ethical views emphasized in this book. Relieving large-scale human suffering is also crucial to prevent atrocities and other disasters. The world is getting smaller and more interconnected. The have-nots are increasingly aware of what the haves have. This kind of knowledge can help to bring down tyrannical regimes; but it can also lead to resentments, and it can be exploited by opportunists in ways that undermine democracy and spawn terrorism.

Global justice is a huge and growing problem. I will make just four brief points here. First, systematic ethical thinking can help us articulate good policies. I offer no overall plan, but surely the prosperous nations, in addition to defending human rights, must give greater support to, and share more with, the poor nations. Second, it is essential that the former be *perceived* as just toward the latter; a good policy that is not properly viewed will not have the effects it should—food and technological support, for example, given into the wrong hands, or in the wrong way, may go unappreciated. Third, the role of international organizations such as the United Nations and the World Court is likely to need expansion if poor and weak nations are to have adequate support in education, population control, health care, and other problems. This expansion is most likely to succeed if individual nations give up sovereignty on some matters, such as their emission of greenhouse gases and the uses of nuclear energy.

My fourth point concerns diplomacy. Relations between the West, especially the United States, and the rapidly growing Islamic world, must be improved. This is not to underemphasize the continuing importance of relations between the West and China and the nations of Africa and South America. But one among other concerns here—and one addressed earlier in connection with religion and politics—is the traditional Islamic rejection of separation of church and state. This rejection has profound implications for the conduct of diplomatic relations, and it raises difficult questions about how democracy may develop in Islamic countries.[25] The Western world cannot help Islamic countries in dealing with the obstacles to democracy that lie here unless more of its leaders achieve a better and wider understanding of Islamic culture and a foreign policy that reflects it. The point may be uncontroversial, but the needed efforts in this direction have only begun.

The Poverty of Communicative Discourse

We come finally to the cluster of problems associated with the commonly low level of discourse in much of the world. This problem is related to that of mental atrophy. Poor literacy is far too common even in such advanced societies as that of the United States. But its mathematical counterpart—*innumeracy*—is even more widespread. Many educational institutions are trying to enhance education in mathematics and science, but it is noteworthy that a large proportion of technically trained people in the United States, at least, come from abroad. Many countries have also not done as well as they should to make mathematics and science attractive to females; even today, both are often perceived as somehow male pursuits.

In an age when the computer should help people to write better (if only because it makes rewriting easy), most educators find writing much weaker than it should be. I refer not just to matters of correct diction and usage but to basic clarity and to the quality of verbal reasoning. Speaking skills are also widely deficient.[26] Here again, role models are important. Especially in the realm of discourse, improving teacher education should help immensely: speaking skills should be emphasized as well as writing and reasoning skills. To support the latter two, we should ask teachers at least from the junior high level upward to achieve at least the equivalent of an arts and sciences major in their subject.

It might seem that in the case of discourse there is nothing we can reasonably hope for in the entertainment media. But that is not so. Granted, characters on the screen should not in general sound more educated than is consonant with their roles. But they also need not sound less so, and there should be just as much entertainment value—and hence just as much profit—in films and television programs done with improvements in the level of speech in these media. (Is it less entertaining, for instance, to have more linguistic variety than one gets with multiply repeated four-letter words?)

In American entertainment, at least, there is also too little of a kind of communication quite important for ethics. Call it *value-sharing discourse*: conversation in which, for instance, people express what they deeply care about, reveal what they think is good or bad, evaluate some of the people or events around them, and share aspirations. This can both reveal character and add dramatic interest. What we often find, by contrast, is male meeting female, a shallow exchange of words, and some plot sequence that reveals little character and much flesh.

The language we speak together—discourse, in one sense—is the main connective tissue of human life. It is pervasive. Part of our problem in this realm is most societies' making too weak a commitment to education. But there is a further problem affecting the education that we do have: a fear that stressing requirements—even a wide set ranging from the humanities and mathematics and languages to the natural and social sciences—is intolerant. But such a grounding in basic methods, subjects, and texts, is not intolerant. Let us celebrate diversity but proceed to appreciate it from the vantage point of a mastery of important material that can serve *any* individual in *any* culture.

A deep knowledge of one's own traditions and culture is by no means narrowing, especially if the traditions are themselves rich and diverse. Indeed, those who do not thoroughly grasp at least one tradition well are ill equipped to understand another. To be sure, the concern with one's own ethnic or national or racial heritage can be pushed too far. It would be unfortunate if we could not enjoy folk music from our own ethnic heritage; but it is probably even worse to be alienated from great music that one might well find even more rewarding simply because it is, say, "Eurocentric."

For all of the ethical problems described in this chapter, I have treated individuals as in a certain way central. Individuals are the prime movers in institutions and the pivotal agents in human history. But many of their significant deeds are mediated—and magnified—by institutions. Moreover, given the place of institutions in the fabric of human culture, and given their role as both preservers of what is valued and agents of change, they are structural foundations for pluralistic democracy.

Here educational institutions play a unique role: they preserve and communicate knowledge; they socialize young adults into responsible citizens; they provide both the stability of connections with the past and the impetus to orderly change when we need it. In them, civic virtue is a complex balance of commitments: to the preservation and generation of knowledge; to the sympathetic presentation of alternative modes of thinking, feeling, and living; to the development of intellectual and moral capacities among students, faculty, and their wider community. Universities should exhibit, in their style and substance, the respect for learning and the intellectual competence that are central to their proper mission.

Parallel points can be made concerning the news media, particularly those not operated for profit. More generally, institutions should not be a cover for individual greed or even a buffer between amoral—or immoral—ambitions and deserved punishment. They should be a means by which human purposes are accomplished through structured collective action. And when we act within them, we are no less human agents governed by moral standards. Institutions, far from protecting immorality, as they have historically so often done, can show morality writ large.

CONCLUSION

Four kinds of ethical view have appeared and reappeared in these pages. The first is virtue ethics, which counsels us to concentrate on *realizing the good* throughout our lives. Here, the fundamental question of ethics is, What should we be like as persons—how should we conceive and cultivate virtues of character and live accordingly? The second and third categories comprise Kantian and intuitionist views; these tell us to concentrate on the *quality of our acts,* though they also take motives into account. For them, the fundamental question of ethics is, What kinds of acts ought we to perform (or avoid)? The Kantian ethic, however, is a master principle view, whereas intuitionist views affirm a plurality of basic moral principles. Utilitarian theories (the fourth category) tell us to *maximize the good.* For them, the fundamental question of ethics is, what kinds of acts tend to *maximize* human happiness? My pluralist universalism, which integrates Kantian, utilitarian, intuitionist, and other elements, stresses all three variables: character, type of action, and overall consequences for happiness.

Each of these ethical views is connected with a theory of value. For virtue ethics, the good is achievement of excellence in thought, action, and character. For Kantian ethics, the dignity of persons and, as a central aspect of it, good will, are the most important (though not the only) values; and

good will is above all a matter of having governing intentions—
those determining one's life plans—that accord with the Categorical Imperative. For classical utilitarianism, pleasure
and pain are the basic positive and negative values. For the
common-sense intuitionist position I have presented, there is
a rich plurality of values. These include values corresponding
to virtue, dignity, and enjoyment; but on my view moral value
has a special place, and there is no closed list of values.
Some are, for instance, distinctively aesthetic, some intellectual, some religious, and some interpersonal in the way that
the values of friendship are.

Each of the ethical views can play an important part in
facilitating a good life. We need not be virtue ethicists to see
the value of achieving excellence. We do not have to be hedonists to consider pleasure a major good in life. And it is
not only Kantians who can regard respecting human dignity
as a central value governing a good life among other people.
Doing so is mainly a matter of treating them as ends in a certain way. Universally valid ethical standards, then, are found
in Aristotle, in Kant, in some of the claims of classical utilitarianism, and (in my view) quite explicitly in the common-
sense moral principles that form the core of a common-
sense intuitionism. This is not to say that any one of these
views encompasses *all* of those standards (though proponents of the views would tend to argue for such comprehensiveness).

On the pluralistic account of value I have presented, radically different kinds of lives can be good. But all good lives
seem to contain, in some proportion, the pleasures of social
interaction, the rewards of excellence in what we are best at,
the exercise of freedom, the animated use of our higher faculties in activities we like, the sense of human dignity in ourselves and others, and, for some people, spiritual satisfactions, whether specifically religious or not. The good life may
be somewhat like nature itself: multifarious in the variety of

its forms, but exhibiting all of them on the basis of some combination of basic elements.

There is no formula for realizing a good life. But this
much can surely be said to suggest where our best hope seems
to lie. We live in a period when the role of universities and
other educational institutions, in countries of all sorts, is pivotal. If we cannot raise the level of discourse and the general
understanding of the world and the disciplines that study it—
including both the humanistic and the mathematical and
scientific—then it is doubtful that people will be sufficiently
responsible citizens in the complex democracies that seem to
be the best political structures for human flourishing, or pro-
ductive enough to maintain an adequate standard of living in
the face of rising world population, growing threats to our
environment, and limited natural resources.

Higher education cannot achieve the needed results
alone. The media play a major part in determining the character of our civilization; business and sports are also influential in shaping our lives; and, for many people, religious institutions are a central element in life. In all of these realms, we
must continue to stress pluralism; but we must not yield to
subjectivism, to indiscriminate relativism, or to a debilitating
skepticism about the value of our traditions. Here, too, the
media should play a constructive part, especially in programming. I am not proposing that we give up a free market in
communication, only that we enhance voluntary exercises of
responsibility.

Institutions are crucial in meeting the ethical challenges
I have stressed, but as important as institutions are, we should
avoid putting disproportionate weight on them. People are
where institutions touch ground. The basic moral thrust and
the good lives that institutions are to serve must be at the
level of individual agents. At this basic level of human action
and interaction, we are not without sound moral principles
or values worth pursuing. I have formulated a number of

these principles and described many of those values. The principles and values we should respect are essential in providing guidance, but they need not hamper our liberty. They provide for great diversity among us without depriving us of common standards of value. The pursuit of justice, freedom, and human flourishing is demanding. But it is possible for all of us together, and the rewards of success are the enduring pleasures of excellence.

NOTES

Chapter 1

1. For discussion of whether science is value-free and of the kinds of value judgments proper to scientific inquiry, see my "Scientific Objectivity and the Evaluation of Hypotheses," in Merrilee H. Salmon, ed., *The Philosophy of Logical Mechanism* (Dordrecht: Kluwer, 1989), pp. 321–345.

2. This is not to say that moral and other value properties cannot have explanatory or perhaps even causal power. The question of whether moral properties have causal power and of what kind of explanatory power they have is pursued in detail in "Ethical Naturalism and the Explanatory Power of Moral Concepts," in my *Moral Knowledge and Ethical Character* (Oxford: Oxford University Press, 1997).

3. William Butler Yeats, "The Second Coming," reprinted in A. J. M. Smith, ed., *Seven Centuries of Verse* (New York: Charles Scribner's Sons, 1957), p. 561.

4. I refer to Aristotle's *Nicomachean Ethics*. For some thorough examinations of the virtue ethics developed there, see John Cooper, *Reason and Human Good in Aristotle* (Cambridge, MA: Harvard University Press, 1975); Alasdair MacIntyre, *After Virtue*, 2nd ed. (Notre Dame: University of Notre Dame Press, 1984); Sarah Broadie, *Ethics with Aristotle* (Oxford: Oxford University Press, 1991); and Julia Annas, *The Morality of Happiness* (Oxford: Oxford University Press, 1993). See also an informative short discussion in provided by Roger Crisp in his introduction to his translation of the *Nicomachean Ethics* (Cambridge: Cambridge University Press, 2000).

5. This generic formulation does not entail the common idea that obligation is *grounded* in divine commands. That version, however, faces the *Euthyphro* problem, so called from Plato's dialogue of that name. In part, the problem is how to rule out the apparent possibility that murder and rape could be obligatory, since, on the face of it, the view that obligation is grounded in divine command does not preclude God's commanding this. I have sketched a more moderate divine command view that avoids the *Euthyphro* problem in "Divine Command Morality and the Autonomy of Ethics," forthcoming in *Faith and Philosophy*. For discussion of divine command ethics and other versions, see Robert M. Adams, *Finite and Infinite Goods* (Oxford: Oxford University Press, 2000), e.g. p. 270. Cf. John Hare: "Divine command theory, as I shall defend it, is the theory that what makes something obligatory for us is that God commands it." See *God's Call* (Grand Rapids, Mich.: William B. Eerdmans: 2001), p. 49.

6. There are also commandments it is natural to call religious, such as the injunction to honor the Sabbath. These may represent moral requirements on the assumption that there is a moral obligation, say a promissory one, to obey God; but the conception of morality operating in this book is non-theological, though readily connected with theological concepts along certain lines. The connection is treated in some detail in my "Religiously Grounded Morality and the Integration of Religious and Political Conduct," *Wake Forest University Law Review* 36, 2 (2001): 251–277. That paper formulates a qualified divine command ethical theory that does not have the repugnant consequence, brought out by Plato's Euthyphro problem, namely that in principle divine command could make murder and rape right.

7. See Immanuel Kant, *Groundwork of the Metaphysics of Morals*, H. J. Paton, trans. (London: Hutchinson, 1961).

8. The notions of treating persons as ends and of treating them merely as means can be clarified even independently of Kant's ethical writings. For an indication of how and references to literature on Kantian ethics, see chapter 3 of my *The Good in the Right: A Theory of Intuition and Intrinsic Value* (Princeton, N.J.: Princeton University Press, 2004).

9. John Stuart Mill, *Utilitarianism*, Oscar Piest, ed. (New York: Macmillan, 1957), p. 10.

10. Mill's quoted formulation is less clear than the formulation I have given in the preceding text; that represents a major kind of utilitarianism—though not the only kind found in Mill—as a sort of *ethics by cost-benefit analysis*: for each of our options, such as giving a donation to *A* versus giving it to *B*, we assign probabilities to relevant outcomes, such as curing someone of malaria, and for each of those outcomes we assign values; we multiply the probabilities by the positive or negative numbers representing the good and bad outcomes, respectively; and we then numerically rank our options accordingly. Right acts are those that maximize the good; they have the highest score in this scheme. What makes this ethics rather than a kind of economics is that it makes goodness, not profit, the standard of conduct.

11. Joseph DesJardins, e.g., in his *Introduction to Business Ethics* 2nd. ed. (Boston: McGraw-Hill, 2005), says, "Utilitarianism is typically identified with the policy of 'maximizing the overall good' or, in a slightly different version, of producing 'the greatest good for the greatest number' " (p. 30). (He does not discuss the difference.) Bentham may be the main source of the greatest number formulation. In his *Introductory View of the Rationale of Evidence*, he says, "Of legislation the proper end may, it is hoped, be stated as being—not but that there are those who will deny it—in every community, *the creation and preservation of the greatest happiness of the greatest number.*" See *The Works of Jeremy Bentham*, John Bowring, ed. (Edinburgh, 1843), sec. 6, pp. 5–6. He does *not*, however, present this as equivalent to his principle of utility: "By the principle of utility is meant that principle which approves or disapproves of every action whatsoever, according to the tendency which it appears to have to augment or diminish the happiness of the party whose interest is in question." See *An Introduction to the Principles of Morals and Legislation* (1989), sec. II.

12. This assumes that the narrow distribution of libraries would not create a degree of resentment that would cause suffering so great as to outweigh the benefits of favoring the educated. Utilitarians always seek to consider the total effect of a possible action;

the point here is that inequality of distribution is not *automatically* or in itself to be avoided. The overall good is the sole standard of conduct.

13. W. D. Ross, *The Right and the Good* (Oxford: Oxford University Press, 1930), pp. 29–30.

14. For a detailed account of Ross's intuitionism and a defense of a view that incorporates major elements of it, see my *The Good in the Right* especially chapters 2 and 3.

15. This contrast is not sharp (and deserves analysis not possible here). Even supposing Kant's formulations of the Categorical Imperative are all equivalent, he appeals (in the intrinsic end formulation of it) to a plurality of moral considerations, e.g. an obligation to avoid treating people merely as means and an obligation (not entailed by that) to treat them as ends. For Mill, too, there is at least the plurality that comes from taking value to have both negative and positive dimensions (those that go with pain and pleasure).

16. The interpretation of justice, freedom, and happiness (and especially the first two) is treated in detail in *The Good in the Right*, especially chapter 5, which also introduces *obligations of manner* as a distinct category. These are not obligations of *matter*—which concern *what* we ought to do—but obligations concerning *how* we should do what we ought to do, e.g. respectfully or generously as opposed to resentfully. The entire set of "Rossian" common-sense obligations may also be integrated under an interpretation of Kant's Categorical Imperative; this *Kantian intuitionism*, as I call it (in chap. 3), is not as easily explained as the pluralist universalism formulated in the text, but the two play similar roles in providing an overarching conception of the kinds of general moral obligations Ross stressed and of many quite specific obligations in daily life.

17. I speak of optimizing rather than maximizing happiness because, for one thing, a maximization standard, even with the limitations the principle expresses, may be too demanding. I also agree with Mill (and Aristotle as I read him) that the quality as well as quantity of happiness is relevant, which makes talk of maximizing happiness at best misleading. I have dealt with this kind of demandingness problem in ethics in, e.g., chapter 4 of *The Good in the Right*. See chapter 5 for rationale for taking freedom to be morally important *independently* of the other Rossian obligations.

18. The problem of deciding just how much one ought to do for others is difficult on any plausible ethical view, and especially for utilitarianism, which makes maximization of the good the central obligation. I have discussed in detail how this problem may be dealt with in chapters 3 and 4 of *The Good in the Right*.

19. I have argued for the unifiability of a broadly Rossian intuitionism by a version of the Categorical Imperative in chapter 3 of *The Good in the Right*.

20. See Thomas Hobbes, *Leviathan* (1651); John Locke, *Second Treatise of Civil Government* (1689), and Jean-Jacques Rousseau, *The Social Contract* (1762). For a contemporary version of a contractualist theory see T. M. Scanlon, *What We Owe to Each Other* (Cambridge, MA: Harvard University Press, 1998).

21. *A Theory of Justice* (Cambridge, Mass.: Harvard University Press, 1971), p. 60. The next few references to Rawls are to this work and will include the relevant page numbers in parentheses. The formulations quoted here, though not unrepresentative, are qualified later in the book.

22. Rawls speaks of primary goods as "things that every rational man is presumed to want" (p. 62). I agree that there are things all rational persons would want but believe this does not follow from the instrumentalist conception of rationality he presupposed and that, like the special assumption concerning envy, it is a substantive idea needed to make the contractarian framework plausible. Much supporting argument for this view is provided in my "Prospects for a Naturalization of Practical Reason: Humean Instrumentalism and the Normative Authority of Desire," *International Journal of Philosophical Studies* 10, 3 (2002): 235–263.

23. This is expectable—though not entailed—by the assumption that moral properties are consequential on natural ("descriptive") ones; e.g. an act is obligatory in virtue ("consequence") of having such descriptive (and non-moral) properties as being an avoidance of hurting someone or as constituting a fulfillment of a promise.

24. Animal rights may be another exception; people seem to disagree on how we may treat them even when they agree on, say, the pain caused by experimentation on them and the resulting benefits to medicine. In both cases, theological facts are relevant (such

as whether under divine law we are stewards of animals), and they can influence even people who have rejected theism.

25. The history of scientific understandings of light is a case in point; wave and particle theories were rationally held by different people at the same time, but no major party to the controversy took the persistence of disagreement to imply that there might be no truth of the matter concerning light.

26. In practice, the same point may hold for divine command theories provided we assume that dignity is God-given. But their *main* point is that rightness is a kind of accord with God's will, and that property, being relational, is not an intrinsic property of the acts in question. So dignity is morally basic only insofar as it reveals God's will.

27. I have not prioritized in any highly specific way, nor said how we should deal with cases in which there is a great gain in utility with the cost of a minor injustice. Here perhaps any theory needs to invoke intuition and Aristotelian practical wisdom.

28. This is meant to recall Mill and indeed Rawls's *Theory of Justice*, but I do not mean to define harm in purely utilitarian terms (there can presumably be moral harms that have no negative effect on happiness), nor to follow Rawls entirely in his view of social justice.

29. The reference is to ratio measurement. Plainly ordinal measurement, which yields only judgments of more or less (or equality), is possible for the properties in question, such as the crucial psychological properties; and, arguably, interval measurement, yielding numbers to represent equal intervals, is possible. Ordinal measurement is apparently all that is strictly needed to sustain my claims in the text.

30. Consider the classical syllogism: All humans are mortal; Socrates is human; hence, Socrates is mortal. This is formally valid (having the form of 'All As are Bs; x is an A; hence, x is a B'), but it is not quantitative (at least not in the way science is, implying ratio measurability of a certain kind as opposed to the quantification required for this kind of syllogism: simply counting and distinguishing between *all* and *some*).

31. Not just anything is permitted by this view. First, if your happiness requires causing my unhappiness, then on the standard

assumption which a happiness principle makes, you may not do the nasty deed that would please you and harm me; and on my own combined theory, there is a specific prohibition of injustice to others.

32. Reduction of freedom is included in injustice, even though the positive ideals of preserving and promoting freedom are not derivable from that of justice.

33. For a recent wide-ranging discussion of cheating in America and its possible causes, see David Callahan, *The Cheating Culture: Why More Americans Are Cheating to Get Ahead* (New York: Harcourt, 2004).

Chapter 2

1. As utilitarianism is usually characterized, an act producing less overall good than the agent can in the situation would be wrong; hence the notion of supererogation as going beyond the call of duty does not apply. But utilitarians can still use 'supererogation' for cases in which (say) one expends such effort, or takes such risk, that one would not be punishable had one produced less good. The action would, then, go beyond a kind of "enforceable" duty.

2. I am not here assuming that instrumental goodness presupposes intrinsic goodness, but it has been argued that nothing can be good as a means unless something is good in itself, since otherwise the existence of anything of instrumental value would require either an infinite or circular instrumental chain. Either A would be a means to B, B to C, and so on to infinity, or A would be a means to something that is a means to A itself. That is plausible reasoning and has been considered so by most value theorists since Aristotle, who brought this problem out (*Nicomachean Ethics* 1094a); but endorsing this reasoning is not an uncontroversial requirement for speaking of instrumental goodness. My main examples of instrumental goodness, however, will be of the common kind that is subordinate to something of intrinsic value.

3. Instrumental good is generally agreed to be dependent, but there is controversy over whether it depends only on instrumental, above all causal, relations to what it is instrumental to, or also on there being something intrinsically good to which it *ultimately* contributes. Can a pesticide be instrumentally good if it is simply *good*

at killing weeds but there is nothing intrinsically good, such as eating delicious foods, to which it is instrumental? All I can say here is that if the instrumental good need does not depend on intrinsic goodness, then to call something instrumentally good is not ultimately to make a *normative* claim at all.

4. An account of why it is morally more important to reduce suffering than to enhance pleasure is proposed in chapter 5 of *The Good in the Right*. It is also plausible to hold that avoiding the doing of positively wrong deeds is morally more important than failing to do something that is morally good, such as assist someone in need. This is discussed in chapter 3 in connection with Kant's Categorical Imperative as calling on us never to treat people merely as means. For a related discussion, see Bernard Gert, *Morality: Its Nature and Justification* (Oxford: Oxford University Press, 1998).

5. This view is developed and defended in my *The Architecture of Reason* (Oxford: Oxford University Press, 2001).

6. Which of these notions is more fundamental: should we analyze intrinsic goodness in terms of contribution to a good life, or vice versa? Perhaps we can do either; my preference is for taking the notion of intrinsic goodness as prior, and in clarifying the notion I offer not a definition, but a theory, of intrinsic goodness. I clarify it by examples, such as the kinds of rewarding experiences we have in human relations and aesthetic appreciation, and seek to understand the good life in terms of appropriate realization of such types of experience.

7. I have explicated inherent value and its relation to intrinsic value in "Intrinsic Value and Reasons for Action," *Southern Journal of Philosophy* 41 Supplement (2003): 30–56.

8. On the notion of proper function, Aristotle and Thomas Aquinas are great classical sources. For a recent discussion, see Alvin Plantinga, *Warrant and Proper Function* (Oxford: Oxford University Press, 1993).

9. Percy Bysshe Shelley, "Ozymandias," in A. J. M. Smith, ed., *Seven Centuries of Verse* (New York: Charles Scribner's Sons, 1957), pp. 361–362.

10. *The Norton Anthology of Poetry*, Alexander W. Allison et al., eds. (New York: Norton, 1983), p. 811.

11. G. E. Moore, while denying that pleasure is the only intrinsic good, suggested that it might be an element in everything that is intrinsically good. See his *Ethics* (Oxford: Oxford University Press, 1912), p. 148.

12. The notion of meaningful life is an important one that I cannot pursue here, but I have provided an account in "Intrinsic Value and Meaningful Life," *Philosophical Papers* 34, 3 (2005): 331–355 (this issue of the journal is entirely devoted to the topic of meaning in life and has a comprehensive introduction by Thaddeus Metz).

13. In the *Groundwork* (393) Kant went so far as to call good will the only 'unconditional good'. In the context he does not imply that it is the only *intrinsic* good, though he does appear to treat it as the only good that provides a condition for the "worthiness" to have a happy life.

14. Avoiding painful frustration of desire is another matter; but to take this as intrinsically good is to employ a hedonic standard, not a desire satisfaction standard of the good (or of rational action). An extensive critical discussion of the desire-satisfaction theory of rationality (and of the good) is given in my "Humean Instrumentalism," cited above.

15. It need not be painful, but is properly dislikable.

16. There are, to be sure, limits on *how* unpleasant an experience can be and still be intrinsically good. But if one doubts that there can be some mixture, consider the sense of doing justice in giving just grades even if it hurts to give students one greatly appreciates only Bs.

17. David Hume, "Of the Standard of Taste," reprinted in Mark Schorer, Josephene Miles, and Gordon McKenzie, eds., *Criticism: The Foundations of Modern Literary Judgment* (New York: Harcourt, Brace, and World, 1958), p. 446.

Chapter 3

1. Doing what I morally should do for the right reason requires more than my merely doing it, but even doing it for the right reason is not sufficient for doing it in the right *manner*. There are different ways to do the same thing for the same reason. Let the act be laying

off an employee, and let the reason be financial emergency; one can lay off the employee gently and sympathetically or curtly and distantly. The concept of duties of manner—*adverbial duties*, we might say (a concept not in general adequately described or emphasized in the literature of ethics)—is treated in detail in chapter 5 of *The Good in the Right*.

2. I might have said 'in facts about the natural world', but that would be unnecessarily controversial. For a defense of the view that the grounding thesis I suggest is plausible and is compatible with a version of divine command theory, see my "Religiously Grounded Morality," *Wake Forest Law Review* (2001).

3. There are exceptions in very unusual circumstances; e.g., it could be necessary to flog someone to save the person from death owing to fear of the devil. But even here we would be obligated to flog minimally and to try to help with the apparent paranoia later.

4. In principle, biotechnology could advance to a point at which any of us could be partially "copied" or even duplicated in a way that produces an adult who is highly or even exactly similar to us. Ethics would not allow us to discriminate on the basis of artificial origin any more than on the basis of race. But what would be the family and social relations of such persons, and who would be responsible for assuring their rights? There are good reasons to avoid cloning human beings at any stage, but the issue is too complex for detailed treatment here.

5. Aristotle says, e.g., that our good (happiness) is the active exercise of the mind (a) in accordance with excellence or virtue, or (b) if there are several virtues, in conformity with the best and most perfect among them, which is "contemplation" (*Nicomachean Ethics* 1098a, Rackham trans. In Irwin's translation, cited earlier, we have: "The human good proves to be the soul's activity in accord with virtue, and indeed with the best and most complete virtue if there are more virtues than one.")

6. Consider, e.g., his analogy of the harper in *Nicomachean Ethics* 1098a, which stresses that the function of a thing is to be determined by reference to an excellent specimen and concludes with the statement quoted in note 5. It is possible that Aristotle thought of complexity (as Mill may have) as an essential or at any rate normal accompaniment of excellent activity and perhaps as a variable

comparable in importance for ranking excellences with their distinctiveness relative to our nature.

7. Mill's emphasis on the role of the higher faculties is evident in several places in chapter 2 of *Utilitarianism*; cf. what John Rawls, in *A Theory of Justice*, calls "The Aristotelian Principle" (p. 426).

8. Mill, *Utilitarianism*, chapter 2 (p. 12).

9. Fortunately not all pleasures we are considering need be sampled: some would obviously lead to death, and many can be adequately assessed by using such common-sense inductive procedures as analogy. If, e.g., eating a few delicious wild mushrooms makes one very sick, eating twice as many may cause death.

10. I bypass here a serious difficulty for utilitarian theories: how to explain why, in a world like this, we can properly do much *other* than promote the goodness of persons overall, even at the cost of doing little or nothing to make our own lives enjoyable. In chapter 3 of *The Good in the Right* I address this difficulty in some detail.

11. As noted in chapter 2, I do not take Kant's claim that good will is the only thing unqualifiedly good to imply that it is the only *intrinsic* good.

12. In chapter 6 of *The Architecture of Reason* (Oxford, 2001) I discuss the status of moral reasons in some detail.

13. For a partial account of treating persons merely as means and as ends, with discussion of Kant's understanding of these notions (though they are characterized independently of his treatment of them), see chapter 3 of *The Good in the Right*.

14. *Groundwork* (399). Kant does, in the context, leave open that the duty may be indirect, "for discontent with one's state . . . might easily become a great *temptation to the transgression of duty*" (ibid.); but he also indicates, here and elsewhere, that pursuing happiness is natural and also befitting to a good life.

15. Chapter 2 of my *Practical Reasoning and Ethical Decision* (New York: Routledge, 2005) explores how Kantian ethics might require engaging in such reasoning, and chapter 5 considers how acting for reasons is possible (even where the reasons are complex) without a process of practical reasoning (this allows that, for retrospective reconstruction of the practical thinking that underlies the action, the reasoning must be in some sense available to the agent for, say, explaining why the action was performed).

16. It an interesting question whether the sense in which we are to love ourselves is supposed to be exactly the sense in which we are to love our neighbors. If so, then 'self-love' may not be the right word for the relevant self-referential attitude and 'respectfully care about' may be a better expression than 'love' for the other-regarding attitude in question. There are both ethical and theological issues here.

17. Love is also not acquirable by coming to have a suitably long-standing and strong set of desires and beliefs in the way that traits of moral character normally are. In "Responsible Action and Virtuous Character," in my *Moral Knowledge and Ethical Character* (Oxford: Oxford University Press, 1997), I have discussed the extent to which such traits are, or at least depend on, desires and beliefs.

18. A detailed case for overlap in major ethical standards among the world's religious can be found in Brian Lepard, *Rethinking Humanitarian Intervention* (College Park: Pennsylvania State University Press, 2002). An informative short description of significant overlap is provided by Patrick E. Murphy et al., *Marketing Ethics* (Upper Saddle River, N.J.: Prentice-Hall, 2005), pp. 35–40.

19. In *The Good in the Right* (esp. chaps. 1 and 2), I have argued that moral principles are knowable through the use of reason, and in *Religious Commitment and Secular Reason* (Cambridge: Cambridge University Press, 2000), especially chapter 5, I have argued that their rational knowability is to be expected in a world under God.

20. It is difficult to say what kind of priority this is. It would not be *automatic* priority. For one thing, our justification for believing such self-evident principles is defeasible. In addition, it may not be self-evident, or even clear to us, that they *are* self-evident. And finally, when there is a conflict of obligations, it will in general *not* be self-evident which predominates. All three points are argued in chapter 2 of *The Good in the Right*.

21. Aquinas says, e.g., "The precepts of the natural law are to the practical reason what the first principles of demonstration are to the speculative reason, because both are self-evident principles," where one of these is that *"good is to be done and promoted, and evil is to be avoided"* (*Summa Theologica*, 2nd Article). It is clear in the context that he is thinking of these self-evident propositions as broadly "analytic" in a sense implying that they are necessary truths.

22. It is a difficult question whether a measure of altruism is required, or at least demanded, by reason, as opposed to a significant amount of other-regarding conduct being required by morality. For a case that reason, in a certain kind of life, demands a measure of altruism and so supports including a certain degree of it in any good life, see my *Architecture*, chapter 6.

23. I should reiterate in this context that a case can be made for treating all of the apparently non-hedonic values as really matters of pleasure or pain; but although a sophisticated hedonic view is plausible, I think we obtain greater clarity and do better justice to the diversity of the facts if we recognize other basic values. That hedonism as normally construed is too narrow a theory of value is argued in *Architecture*, chapter 6.

24. A detailed discussion of the good life and its connection with meaningfulness in life—*existential meaningfulness*—is provided in my "Intrinsic Value and Meaningful Life," *Philosophical Papers* 34, 3 (2005): 331–355.

25. To be sure, there can be unique satisfactions in the rectification of evil as opposed to the more positive gratification that often comes with doing the kinds of good things that do not presuppose any evils to be undone. The examples in the text are only a brief indication of coherence-making elements in a good life.

26. A prominent kind of vision of how a liberal democracy is constituted is found in John Rawls, *The Law of Peoples* (Cambridge, Mass.: Harvard University Press, 1999).

Chapter 4

1. John Rawls calls an institution "a public system of rules which define offices with their rights and duties, powers and immunities, and the like." See *A Theory of Justice*, p. 55. This applies widely, but consider private institutions. Must their rules be public? Moreover, this characterization suggests a mainly internal focus and also says nothing explicitly about a unifying set of purposes, something an institution must have.

2. The rules may have to include criteria for membership or participation, and these might have to be of the kind one can satisfy by voluntary behavior as opposed to, say, heredity. But here I leave this issue aside. Note that institutions characteristically have a

history; but a university can presumably be an institution at the moment of its founding, *before* it has a history.

3. One might want to rule out certain kinds of goals and thus eliminate, say, commercial entities, or at least those with *only* commercial purposes, but I leave open that some organizations run for profit may nonetheless count as a kind of institution.

4. One could make an exception for the bare possibility that an institution has always existed, but there is no reason to think that any institution we know of *is* without beginning.

5. For a technologically sophisticated treatment of institutional concepts, see Raimo Tuomela, *Cooperation* (Dordrecht: Kluwer, 2000).

6. If they didn't, and an exactly similar entity was created, would we have a re-establishment of the same institution but not know it, or just the founding of an exactly similar one? This bears considerable thought, but may be left open here.

7. There are different senses in which an institution can be public, e.g. publicly chartered and funded as opposed to operating in public, as does a commercial corporation by contrast with a private club.

8. This point is supported in my *Religious Commitment and Secular Reason* (New York: Cambridge University Press, 2000), especially chapter 2, which discusses all three principles in the context of the theory of the basis of free democracy.

9. We cannot plausibly hold that preference for some one denomination entails establishment of it; but it tends in that direction and would be objectionable on similar grounds, such as encouraging discrimination against denominations not favored by the government.

10. For an extensive and legally informative discussion of the question whether teaching intelligent design is constitutional in the United States, see Kent Greenawalt, *Does God Belong in Public Schools?* (Princeton, N.J.: Princeton University Press, 2005).

11. Aquinas held something like this, believing that the basic moral principles can be ascertained through the use of reason—a point detachable from the natural law framework in which he (at least mainly) applied it. The issue here is the epistemic autonomy of ethics.

12. The mandate or requirement is only prima facie if it is not always rational on balance to be moral *and* our rationality is, as it seems, our basic guiding light. There are difficult issues here in both ethical theory and philosophy of religion.

13. The principle of secular rationale does not entail that one must disclose one's vote. First, one can offer a reason for voting a given way without implying that one will so vote, or has so voted; second, one overrider of the prima facie obligation to offer a reason might be a need to keep one's vote secret. This principle is explicated and defended at length in my *Religious Commitment and Secular Reason,* chapters 4–6. A later treatment that meets objections to the principle not addressed in the book is provided in my "Moral Foundations of Liberal Democracy, Secular Reasons, and Liberal Neutrality Toward the Good," *Notre Dame Journal of Law, Ethics and Public Policy* 19, 1 (2005): 197–218.

14. An interesting question, put to me by Kent Greenawalt, is whether reasons presupposing atheism are ruled out as (I take it) religious in the broad sense that they directly concern religion. I have not construed such reasons as religious in the ordinary sense, but they are at least not *religiously neutral,* and on that ground may be objectionable in certain ways in a liberal democracy. This accounts for part of the wording of the principle of secular rationale.

15. I have stated and given a preliminary defense of this principle in "Religiously Grounded Morality and the Integration of Religious and Political Conduct," *Wake Forest University Law Review* 36, 2 (2001): 251–277.

16. The principles of secular and religious rationale may also be applied to the abortion issue, but that is even more complicated than the assisted suicide question, in part because the former raises the metaphysical question of what constitutes a human person (this is not the same as the vague question "when human life begins," which applies to biological entities that are only very controversially considered persons). These principles are applied to the abortion issue, in the context of many arguments for and against the permissibility of abortion, in chapter 7 of *Religious Commitment and Secular Reason.*

17. In "Tolerance without Relativity: A Perspective on Moral Education" (ms.) I discuss this and connect it with the fourth-grade

"Fact and Opinion" Unit used by Lincoln, Nebraska, Public Schools at least from the mid-1970s through the mid-1980s.

18. Some aspects of preselecting the sex of children are treated in a *New York Times* article of July 4, 2004.

19. In Alexander W. Allison et al., eds., *The Norton Anthology of Poetry*, 3rd ed. (New York: W.W. Norton, 1983), pp. 1181–1182. The poem was written in 1951 during the time of Thomas's father's final illness.

20. Ibid., pp. 996 and 997.

21. That our moral responsibilities demand more of us than simply acting within our rights is argued in my "Wrongs within Rights," *Philosophical Issues* 15 (2005): 121–139.

22. A related problem is discretion in making private life public. Does the public need to hear so much about sexual indiscretions if they do not bear on capacity to do the relevant job? Arguably, Martin Luther King was hypocritical in being a Christian minister yet committing adultery (assuming he in fact did); but this may depend on how he represented himself (say, as a sinner rather than self-righteously or as a model Christian). One can be a model in more than one domain, of course. Perhaps a key point is that we should not try to be public models in areas where our private life would undermine our credibility.

23. In "The Function of the Press in a Free and Democratic Society," *Public Affairs Quarterly* 4 (1990): 203–215.

24. To judge, however, by a report by sports commentator Frank De Ford (National Public Radio, April 4, 2001), one opportunity is being lost: he cited a number of respects in which women's athletics is exhibiting the same ethically unacceptable practices (e.g., discrimination, "fixing" of outcomes, and commercialism) found in men's athletics.

25. Technically, at least, England does not separate church and state, so it should not be argued that democracy cannot work without (full) separation.

26. Consider a prominent or even growing trend, especially among the young, and apparently more among females than males, that we might call *interrogativizing the declarative*. I'm referring to that raised inflection of the voice coming at the end of a statement and often making it sound like a question. I have heard it even when

people tell me their names. I have heard it when someone says to a person telephoning, e.g., "This is Dr. A's office calling?" And I have heard it as people lay out directions, such as "when you get to the corner of Fifteenth Street?" Why should we care? Because the interrogative inflection already has an important role that it cannot play as well if we use it for an entirely different purpose. Because we will produce even more misunderstandings than we already do if inflection is not used to support meaning. Because these interrogatives add a note of unsureness, even timidity, which is often inappropriate to the statement and context—and may harm women by reinforcing stereotypes we should try hard to bury. And because misleading language and poor articulation of our messages tend to cause sloppiness of thought. I do not know how the trend arose, but I suspect that some media figures with whom younger people identify have made it attractive. I doubt the trend is being consciously encouraged. But follow-the-leader can be a bad game even when one knows who the leader is and why one is following. Interrogativizing the declarative (sometimes called "upspeak") has no known leaders, no apparent rationale, and too many unwitting followers.

INDEX

Adams, Robert M., 124n5
altruism, 63, 135n22
Annas, Julia, 123n4
Aquinas, Thomas, Saint. *See*
    Thomas Aquinas, Saint.
Aristotle, 5–7, 13, 27, 66–68, 70,
    71, 120, 123n4, 126n17,
    129n2, 132nn5,6
assisted suicide, 24, 29, 96, 99,
    137n16
autonomy, 85, 90
    of ethics, 136n11

basic value. *See* value, basic.
beneficence, 14, 16, 18, 24, 71,
    87, 91, 106
Bentham, Jeremy, 10, 125n11
Bible, the, 8, 12, 13, 73–74, 75,
    98, 99, 107
Brand, Myles, 111
Broadie, Sarah, 123n4

Callahan, David, 129n33
caring, 37, 63, 64
categorical imperative, the, 9–10,
    15, 70–72, 120, 126nn15,16,

130n4. *See also* dignity; Kant;
    respect for persons
celebrity effect, 110
church-state separation.
    See separation of church
    and state
civic virtue, 113
cloning, 29, 65, 99, 100, 101,
    132n4
coherence, 79, 135n25
consequentialism, 23
contractarianism, 18–19, 127n22
Cooper, John M., 123n4
Crisp, Roger, 123n4

De Ford, Frank, 138n24
deontological theories, 23
DesJardins, Joseph, 125n11
dignity, 119, 129, 128n26
duty. *See* obligation

emotion, 45–46, 51, 74
enjoyment. *See* pleasure
Eliot, T. S., 103
ethics, divine command,
    8–9,124n5, 124n6

ethics, institutional, 6, 80, 84,
    86, 94
ethics, journalistic, 89–91
ethics, medical, 44. *See also* cloning
ethics of citizenship, 95–99, 109
ethics of love. *See* love, ethics of
eudaimonia, 66
euthanasia, 14–15
Euthryphro problem, 124n5,
    124n6

fallibilism, 27
fittingness, 38, 39, 50, 133n14
forgiveness, 46
freedom, 17–18, 20, 21, 26, 64, 81,
    97, 107, 108, 126nn16–17,
    129n32
Free Exercise Clause, 29, 93
friendship, 45, 46, 62–63, 64, 65,
    70, 120

Gert, Bernard, 130n4
goodness, 4, 5–7, 27, 28, 36–55,
    62, 68, 79. *See also* valuation
    inherent, 37, 41, 64
    instrumental, 36, 129n2
    intrinsic, 36
    moral, 4, 5
    objective, 27
    organic character of, 49–52
    overall, 42
    primary, 19, 127n22
    unqualified, 70
Greenawalt, Kent, 136n10,
    137n14

happiness. *See* pleasure
Hare, John, 124n5

hedonism, 68–70, 135n23. *See also*
    pleasure
Hobbes, Thomas, 18
Hume, David, 54, 62

inherent value. *See* value,
    inherent
institutional ethics. *See* ethics,
    institutional
inherent value. *See* value,
    inherent
intrinsic value, 45, 47, 50–53,
    130n7. *See also* goodness,
    value
intuitionism, viii, 11–14, 15, 16,
    89, 120, 126nn14,16,
    127n19
Kantian, 126n16
Irwin, Terence, 66, 132n5

Kant, Immanuel, 9–10, 15, 16, 20,
    48, 60, 70–73, 89, 104–105,
    119, 120, 124n8,
    126nn15–16, 130n4, 131n13,
    133n11, 133nn13–15
Kantian intuitionism. *See*
    intuitionisn, Kantian
King, Martin Luther, 138n22

Lepard, Brian, 134n18
Locke, John, 18
love, 8, 45–46, 62–63, 76,
    134nn16–17
    ethics of, 74–75

MacIntyre, Alasdair, 123n4
master principle theories, 9,
    10, 15

mean, principle of the, 7, 67
Metz, Thaddeus, 131n12
Mill, John Stuart, 10–11, 15, 16,
    27, 28, 47, 68–70, 72,
    125n10, 126n15, 126n17,
    132–33nn6–7
Moore, G. E., 131n11
moral education, 109, 112
moral obligation. See obligation
moral rights. See rights
moral value. See goodness;
    intrinsic value
moral virtue. See virtue ethics
multiculturalism, 27, 98,
    106–107
Murphy, Patrick E., 134n18

obligation, viii, 12–14, 15, 16, 17,
    20, 27, 54, 55, 59–60, 71–72,
    78, 124n5, 124n6
    final, 13
    institutional, 87–89, 94, 113
    of manner, 126n16
    of matter, 126n16
    prima facie, 13
organicity (of value), 50–51.
    See also goodness

pain. See pleasure
Plantinga, Alvin, 130n8
Plato, 5, 124nn5, 6
pleasure, 10–11, 13, 23, 28, 37,
    41–42, 43, 44, 45, 46, 47,
    48–49, 63, 67, 68–70, 79, 80,
    104, 120, 130n4, 131n11,
    133n9, 135n23
pluralism, 61, 67, 78, 80, 83, 105.
    See also goodness

institutional, 83
moral, 59–81
practical wisdom, 6, 7, 13, 66, 67,
    70, 72, 96, 128n27
prima facie duty. See obligation,
    prima facie
principle of the mean. See mean,
    principle of the
proxy rights principle, 99

rational disagreement, 21–22
Rawls, John, 18–19, 127nn21–22,
    128n28, 133n7, 135n26,
    135n1 (chapter 4)
relativism, viii, 24–6, 61, 109
    circumstantial, 25
    preferential, 80
    status, 25, 78, 107
repentance, 51, 60
respect for persons, 10, 72, 111.
    See also dignity
rights, 20, 29, 65, 76, 99, 100,
    132n4, 138n21
    animal, 127n24
    human, 105–106, 113
    proxy, 99
    secondary, 99
Ross, W. D., 12–14, 18, 20,
    66, 77, 78, 91 126n14,
    126n16
Rousseau, Jean-Jacques, 18
rule ethics, 7–13

Salmon, Merilee H., 123n1
Scanlon, T. M., 127n20
separation of church and state,
    92–95
Shakespeare, William, 44, 60

Shelley, Percy Bysshe, 43, 45, 55
sports, 28, 32, 40, 48, 67, 68, 79,
    111–112, 121, 138n24
supererogation, 35, 60, 129n1

teleological theories, 23
theo-ethical equilibrium, 77
Thomas, Dylan, 103, 138n19
Thomas Aquinas, Saint, vii, 77,
    130n8, 134n21, 136n11
Tuomela, Raimo, 136n5

United Nations, 113
universalizability, 10, 73. See also
    categorical imperative
utilitarianism, 10–11, 15, 16, 17,
    18, 23–24, 35, 72, 89, 105,
    113, 119, 120, 125nn10–11,
    125n12, 127n18, 128n28,
    129n1 (chapter 2), 133n10

valuation, 36–37, 41, 62
value, 3–5, 37–56, 61–62, 95,
    119–120, 123nn1–2, 125n10,
    129n2, 129n3
    aesthetic, 43–45
    basic, 79
    hedonic, 42, 68–70, 135n23
    inherent, 40–41, 64, 130n6
    instrumental, 37, 38, 47, 129n2
    intrinsic. See intrinsic goodness
    moral, 47–49, 50
    spiritual, 45
    See also goodness
valuing, 37–39, 40, 63
virtue. See Aristotle; civic virtue;
    love; virtue ethics
virtue ethics, 5–7, 14, 15, 17, 31,
    74–76, 102, 119, 123n4

Yeats, William Butler, 4